CONTENTS

DEDICATION

MY SECOND-FAVORITE TRIVIA QUESTION IS: WHO WROTE THE lyrics for the theme song to *Exodus,* the movie based on the Leon Uris novel about the founding of Israel?

No, not Herbert Gold, he wrote that nice Jewish *music.*

I'm talking about those nice Jewish *lyrics.*

Here's the answer:

Pat Boone.

(My *very* favorite trivia question is: who has the patent on the first mechanical heart? The answer is the ventriloquist and voiceover actor who created Jerry Mahoney and immortalized Tigger: Paul Winchell.)

Anyway, when I was a kid, I was browsing through the local library, and there was this 1959 book by ol' white shoes, the Boonester, himself. It was a book of advice for adolescents and teens, called *Twixt Twelve and Twenty.* I was straitlaced enough not to need his advice on clean livin', thank you very much, but books by celebrities are always interesting to look at, even if only to try to guess from the style whether they were ghosted, so out of curiosity I picked it up, paged through it, and stopped at Pat's dedication page.

On it was an invitation for the reader to write his or her name on a blank line he'd provided. I'm paraphrasing the words, but not the sentiment, which was *I want you to know, every time you turn to this page, that the book you're holding is just for you.*

I thought that was a little too cornball to be believed, rolled my eyes or something, and put the book back on the shelf. I've never seen a copy of it since.

But I've never forgotten that page either.

And having just put the finishing touches on my *own* book of advice, I find myself having a lot more respect for Mr. Boone's gesture. Suddenly I don't think it's all that damn cornball. Suddenly I think he had a point. And I think he meant it with all his heart. I hope so. Because now I believe I know what he was feeling.

If you aspire to write musicals, write them well and write them for keeps, you aspire to do something noble and difficult and worthwhile and brave. The craft is complex, the business side requires serious navigation, and it's not an ambition for the faint of heart. If this is your dream, you dream big, and it's a dream that needs encouragement.

So guess what?

I dedicate this book to

_____

Fill in your name.

Because I want you to know—

—every time you turn to this page—

—that the book you're holding is *just for you.*

Okay?

Let's don't get all mushy about it, it's just the way things are.

Oh, and this book is also, with love, for Joan, who kicked my butt and made me write it for you. (And acknowledgments to my pal and colleague Jerry James, whose merciless notes forced me to make it better.)

Given the circumstance, I know you won't mind sharing . . .

FOREWORD

WHEN WE MET DAVID SPENCER IN THE BMI-LEHMAN ENGEL Musical Theatre Workshop, we were a little afraid of him.

First of all, David has the superhuman ability to speak in fully formed, perfect prose sentences. Never a single "uh" or "um." It's disconcerting. And the sentences would always add up to paragraphs, each with its own clear point, and each point working to support the main thesis idea. And the main thesis idea was, usually, that your song didn't work.

And he was usually right.

Second, David seemed to have all of musical theatre history at his fingertips—he could pull any example out of the air to illustrate his points. All of a sudden he'd start quoting Lehman Engel, Ed Kleban, or Howard Ashman, or talking about some obscure Jones and Schmidt production from the seventies, and you'd think, "Fuck—how can I compete with that?"

Third, David knew all the rules about musical theatre writing. He'd been in the Workshop for a long time. We're not even sure how long. And he would throw these rules at you by means of these quippy little turns of phrase, like "that's not your friend." He would never say, "Your main character should never seem self-pitying." He'd say "Your main character is self-pitying, and that's not your friend."

So we were a little terrified of him. At first.

What was really going on was that David was being a perceptive, analytical, honest critic—and everyone, deep down, is scared of criticism. You're always scared that some insightful person will be able to poke a hole in your work and publicly expose you as the fraud you are.

But criticism is very, very good for your craft. David's honest commentary was one of the many factors that helped us make *Avenue Q* better and better. We brought about three-fourths of the songs from the score of *Avenue Q* in to BMI to try them out, and believe us, we did a ton of rewrites. The more scrutiny a piece is subjected to, the more objections raised, the more help the writers have in fortifying the craft so that, once it's done, it's far stronger than before it went through the fire.

Writers often have a resistance to learning the rules when they're starting out. They feel true creativity lies in free-form expression. But what are rules? Rules are the collected wisdom of the entire history of the artists working in the form. And that's something you should bother to learn before you start departing from it.

In the end, we got over our fear of David and discovered he was actually a really friendly, sweet, humorous guy. To adapt one of his favorite phrases, he's our friend. And, if you can't come to New York and join the BMI Workshop and meet him for yourself, this book is definitely the next best thing.

—*Robert Lopez*
Jeff Marx

ACKNOWLEDGMENTS AND DEEP GRATITUDE

FIRST AND FOREMOST TO MY FAMILY—MOM, DAD, BROTHER Steven—without whose unstinting love and support I simply could not have survived in the theatre or anywhere else—and the family that has made me an overjoyed member, thanks to Joan: the prolific and wonderful Delahunt clan, overseen by their warm, energetic, and intrepid matriarch, Margaret.

Thanks next to the BMI-Lehman Engel Musical Theatre Workshop, which has provided a spiritual home, a nurturing ground, many of the most profound relationships of my life, and since the late '80s, a good part of my career, too. Indeed, it was the opportunity to write for and edit the Workshop newsletter that made me realize I'd been writing a book all along. Special thanks to my stalwart colleagues on the Steering Committee, currently Jean Banks, Maury Yeston, Patrick Cook, Frederick Freyer, Richard Engquist, Nancy Golladay, Jane Smulyan, and Frank Evans. A grateful nod to *ex officios* Susan Schulman, Skip Kennon, Ellen Fitzhugh, the late Ed Kleban, and the late Allan Becker as well.

For the wisdom and guidance of great teachers who have also been good friends and mentors, thanks to Stephen Sondheim, the late novelist Walter Wager, and my late manager Scott Shukat.

For opportunities to develop as a writer over the long haul, appreciation to Jim Morgan at the York Theatre, Theatreworks/USA, the Richard Rodgers Foundation, and especially Sondra Gilman and Celso Gonzalez-Falla.

Penultimately, a list of people I adore, who changed my life for the better, all of whom know why I adore them personally and professionally: Lisbeth Lloyd, Rebecca Edmonston, Maryrose Wood (and Harry and Beatrix), Judith Thiergaard, Adele Ahronheim, Robert Viagas, Melissa Collins, Joe Gianono, Daniel Marcus, Laura Stanczyck, Jenny Giering, Stephen Terio, Fred Lassen, Sheryl Kaller, John Vornholt, Stephen Witkin, Rob Barron, Alan Brennert, Austin Pendleton, and Alan Menken.

For my introduction to the editor, my friend and supporter, the renowned playwright and teacher, Jeffrey Sweet.

And finally, because she wanted this book for Heinemann, and then edited it more brilliantly and sensitively than I dared hope, Lisa Barnett.

INTRODUCTION

AS THIS BOOK GOES TO PRESS, I WOULD PRAGMATICALLY describe myself as a musical dramatist with a solid reputation and cult notoriety. I have enough cast albums and selectively distributed album-quality demos to my credit to have gotten my work Out There to a decent if modest degree; enough significant productions on my resume to mark me a Serious Player; enough prestigious musical theatre awards to signify that I'm good at what I do; and a consistently active public professional history, from 1984 to the present. I'm on the Steering Committee of the BMI-Lehman Engel Musical Theatre Workshop where I teach as cochair of the Second Year Songwriters class and also moderate the Master Class program, I screen for various musical theatre grant-and-development organizations, and I hire out for private script consultations.

All of which sounds pretty good—and after a fashion, it is.

But like most people who'd call themselves professional musical dramatists, what I'm after is the brass ring: Broadway credentials, shows that are a ubiquitous part of the repertoire, and yes, the modest notoriety that comes with.

Oddly, though, it may be my "midlist" status (to borrow a publishing term) that best qualifies me to write this book.

Because in an industry that seems sometimes *built* to defeat anyone foolhardy enough to enter it, I've survived *steadily*—and most times managed to make my living at it.

And that's what this book is about: the ability to *keep going*. To get the work produced, performed, recorded, published, licensed, appreciated—*seen*. To make the most of the opportunities that come your way and generate your own opportunities too. And to do it consistently. So that you can feel good about the musical theatre journey you're on, so that you win more than you lose, so that the work feels worthwhile and enriching. So that you can walk proud like the accomplished professional you (hopefully) are; and not keep tilting at windmills like the gifted hobbyist circumstance and defenselessness might otherwise leave you feeling. So that, whether you achieve the brass ring or not, you can at least remain a viable, visible, valued practitioner.

Come to think of it, maybe that's the *other* brass ring. . . .

I suspect that by now I'd be far higher up on the food chain, too, were it not for mistakes I've made along the way. Some of them due to growing-up/personality glitches, some of them due to naïveté and inexperience, some of them having to do with putting my trust in the wrong place, bending to an unhealthy political pressure, etc. etc. The *usual* list of reasons. The list that almost *everyone* in our business has acquired, in individual ways.

As I've compared notes over the years with colleagues and contemporaries—including "brand name" veterans—I've come to realize that despite our individual circumstances and personal particulars, we've all been prey to the same traps, lapses, and betrayals.

You can't avoid them all. No one can. Getting bruised is part of life, unavoidably a part of show business, and it's often the only means by which you learn. The tragedy arises when bruising becomes *the dominant force* in how you learn. Because so many mistakes, missteps, false lures—*so* many—are avoidable.

But not without some foreknowledge. The geography of the biz is complex, and while instinct is invaluable, it can get confused by a welter of incoming data that you can't properly analyze because, to paraphrase Meredith Willson, you don't know the territory.

Certainly *I* didn't, when I started. And it took a long time to become conversant. (And the business has only gotten harder over the years, for nearly everyone from the postgraduate wannabe right up through Stephen Sondheim.)

But if anything has kept me *afloat* over the years, it's that I've given most of the entries on the aforementioned list—the list of reasons why/how mistakes get made—an iconic significance. Rather than just view a disappointing event or circumstance as part of my history, I've looked for the larger, universal implication. The *lesson*. Not just the disciplinary lesson, the personal lesson, the lesson about "the other guy" who sabotaged a worthy effort—but the *procedural* lesson. Even the ethics lesson, if there is one (especially if it applies to *my* behavior). The lesson that turns a misadventure into a guiding principle for the future. For I've found that with every bad situation I've known—always—somewhere early, a little red warning flag popped up. And if I didn't read it or see it, or give it due significance, it's because I was too blinded by other factors—hunger, fear, intimidation, innocence—to *want* to do so.

As I further compared my good and bad experiences with the more famous successes and disasters that populate musical theatre history, the revelation came that there were *patterns* informing good and bad experiences on *every* level.

Once I learned to read the signs, the people, and the politics, my road became smoother, my progress faster, sometimes astonishingly so.

And that's part of what this book is about: providing a road map for the aspiring, even the experienced, musical dramatist, so that you make your choices wisely, as relates to people, procedures, venues, and politics. And, of course, the art.

But this book is about much more than that.

There's something else that's kept me afloat. And it's this: I've gotten a lot of stuff right, too.

And similarly, when I stumbled upon something new that worked more than once, performed a particular sort of industry kindness that karmically "came back" to me in a positive way, "discovered" a principle that I had never known to be codified or otherwise articulated before . . . I took note of that, too.

I realized the value in being a stickler for presentation; I became rigorous about deconstructing every musical I knew or saw, to understand the ways in which it did and didn't work, commercially and artistically . . . and realized there were even some standard principles and procedures of craft—not to mention attitude—that, again, had somehow avoided formal presentation in a book dedicated to imparting "secrets" of the trade. By a professional, for professionals—and those who sincerely desire to be. [1]

---

1. I pause here to acknowledge, with deep respect, *Making Musicals* by master lyricist-librettist Tom Jones. A lovely little volume, its focus, even by dint of its subtitle ("An Informal Introduction to the World of Musical Theatre"), is that of a rudimentary primer, more than a survival manual. Its purpose, and the purpose of this book, don't overlap by very much. (More on Mr. Jones' book is in Appendix III.)

Some of these "secrets" are basic "holy writ," some are philosophical truisms, but *all* have, or relate to, solid, practical application. These are your lifelines.

Within, you will find several kinds of chapters. They delve variously into aspects of art, craft, presentation, venue, situation, and politics. There's also an appendix containing two of the theatre reviews I've written for my web 'zine *Aisle Say*, as samples of the kind of deconstructive analysis you can do to help inform your own work. An additional appendix includes a personal reading list: further info to round everything out.

Regarded as a whole, this is a constructive view from the trenches, a lighthouse made of print, for those who venture as writers into Musical Theatre Land.

Notwithstanding the format and equipment sections, which are pretty nuts-and-bolts, and the identification of essential craft principles, you will inevitably find points in this book (though I hope not *too* many) where you feel, *Well, that's about Spencer's experience, and it applies not at all to me.* And perhaps you'll be right. But understand, I'm less concerned with your taking every bit of advice rigorously to heart than I am with how you create a mental/emotional/procedural/craft-based mechanism *that allows you to respond to the business in the healthiest way for* you. If you start with this as a basis, trust your gut, and adapt appropriately as you make your way, you shouldn't go far wrong.

And with that said: relax. Take a deep breath and take heart. You don't have to work without a net anymore. Read what follows, and you'll find that both the craft and the business—and what you need to consider in order to make your way through them—will seem a lot less daunting.

Stick around a while . . . and then stick around a while. . . .

1

CHAPTER

You're Only as Good as Your Partner —and Vice Versa or: Collaboration

HOW ABOUT DINNER AND A MOVIE SOMETIME?

COLLABORATION, THE CLICHÉ GOES, IS LIKE MARRIAGE; BUT I find that to be a misleading homily. The marriage part doesn't come until much later.

At first, collaboration is like dating. And I mean *exactly* like dating.

After long, hard experience, and more youthful mistakes than I care to think about, I've come to realize that I can determine after one meeting (usually within a few *minutes* of one meeting), whether I want to see the person again in a collaborative context, and indeed whether or not I *should*. It's not always a determination that comes with any facts or objective truths attached. Nor does it matter how talented—or even well-intentioned and pleasant—the other person is; if there's no personal synergy between us, I'm outta there: life's too short, and the work's too hard. Like most experienced people, I'm attuned to *obvious* danger signs—manipulative tactics, intellectual laziness, lack of enthusiasm and/or preparation, grandstanding, false pretensions of intimacy, disingenuousness, etc.—but as often as not, the signals are inexplicable in any rational sense. It's a reading from my intuition . . . what I call my antenna. Every time I've trusted it, things worked out well. Anytime I've tried to resist it, I wound up in trouble. And the same seems to have been true for virtually every other writer I've spoken to on the subject.

That said, there is a practical caveat: let's say you're a relatively unknown writer and you suddenly get the opportunity to test-run a collaboration with someone on the A-list—an experienced, renowned and *universally acknowledged* Broadway veteran. And let's say this guy is more neurotic than you're comfortable with, or doesn't get your sense of humor, or whatever. Obviously, you'd be crazy not to try the collaboration on for size, not to do everything within reason to make it work. But remember, this A-list player is no less human than the unknown writer you rejected for the same reason. Chemistry is chemistry no matter *what* the stakes are; and you must further deal with the political reality: the veteran is higher up on the food chain than you are and there may not be parity where creative power or influence is concerned. There may be other factors at play that mitigate these concerns—perhaps the director brought you into the project, or something like that—but if your instinct says the odds are too heavily stacked against a healthy working environment (not your insecurity or your stage fright or some niggling apprehension that you might not deliver the goods—that's normal—but your *survival* instinct), save yourself the time and the heartache and *trust the feeling*.

Which brings me to the next hard-won truth. . . .

IT'S NEVER TOO LATE TO BAIL

At least, not until the contracts are signed and you're in the land of legal commitments. But until that point, if you find yourself in a dysfunctional relationship, or laboring to make viable a project (or an approach) that you don't believe in, *nothing stops you from jumping ship*. I have heard more writers than I can remember say that they'll stay with a doomed project or an impossible collaborator because *they've invested so much time . . . they've done so much work, some of it really good . . . maybe there's a chance* . . . all boilerplate excuses, and none more valid than those that keep a battered wife going back to an abusive husband—or those of a couple who keep a strained marriage together "for the sake of the children." (Liken the collaborative paradigm to that of a life partner or constant companion. The truths are *precisely* the same.) Bad situations will only worsen exponentially, and any project that goes into production burdened with dysfunction within the creative team is finished before it starts. When there's chronic trouble, follow the advice of that house in *The Amityville Horror* and *get out*.

The dissolution of a collaboration may not always be easy. In many cases, there are questions of project ownership, intellectual property, rights to work that has already been completed, and so on. I won't address those here, for two reasons: (1) Most of the time, the project is so accursed or misconceived that the perceived loss is not worth the battle; (2) I'm not qualified to discuss the legalities of the rare cases where such questions may be legitimate, save to say that collaboration agreements—the industry prenups—can be very helpful. (Though *personally* I have very mixed feelings about them. Such a document can be a Faustian bargain whose price is mutual trust. This is an *extremely tough call*, and *I would never advise any writer to eschew protection.* I can only tell you *I've* never had a fruitful collaboration in which the parties felt it necessary to hammer out written rules of the road. Only the collaborations that failed had collaboration agreements in place. That said, *never refuse a collaborator who requests one,* for that can engender its own distrust. A collaboration agreement, mixed blessing though it may be, is a legitimate request.)

Remember, what's *really* at stake here is your psychological health. The work we do is so personal, and we are so exposed while going through the birth process, that we need to be part of a support system that will nourish and encourage our efforts and enthusiasm as much as possible. Very little takes a hit to your self-esteem and creativity as effectively as an oppressive or negative partnership, or project whose foundation makes you feel insecure.

But let's say you find a collaboration that works. Lucky you. But don't take it for granted.

Any good collaboration requires mutual . . .

MAINTENANCE (INTERNAL)

You and your collaborator(s) represent the primary creative team. That's the nucleus. Everybody else is secondary or tertiary, with the arguable exception of some directors, but that must be determined on a case-by-case basis. This doesn't mean you should keep other personnel at bay, but it's important to have a protected, privileged "space" that is for you and your collaborator(s) alone.

Traditionally there are no more than three people in the primary loop: the composer, the lyricist, the librettist; and no fewer than two, at least one of whom would be a "hyphenate," such as a composer-lyricist or a lyricist-librettist.

Two is easier to maintain than three (or more—for example, when the book is cowritten by a fourth party). The more bodies there are in the mix, the harder it is to keep checks and balances in place. But you must.

Since two-person collaborations are the ones with which I've had the most experience, I'll use that as the template, and touch upon variables introduced by three-or-more later.

Establish early on and with clear, considerate, respectful conversation —and a grace period of trial and error—where the comfortable lines of demarcation between your disciplines lie. There are no hard-and-fast rules here other than the ones you determine among yourselves.

For example: I've had several collaborations in which I was lyricist to other composers. One composer considered it the height of rudeness for me to suggest a rhythmic scan, and held the primacy of the composer to decide *anything* musical as an inviolate principle. Another composer quickly came to the conclusion that the patterns in which I conceived lyrics—since I am myself a composer—were too idiosyncratic to impose his will upon; he just flat-out asked me what style of music I had in mind and to read the lyric out loud in strict, time-signatured rhythm; he had the power of veto and sometimes used it, but not before considering the alternative.

All librettists are different, too. I've worked with one who didn't want me to invent *any* dialogue; another who encouraged me to noodle and rearrange, not wanting to second-guess the precise nuances of book-into-song integration; another who was mildly proprietary but never said "no" when I asked, "Do you mind if I sketch something out here, 'cuz I think it'll be clearer than if I try to describe it?"

What's important is not a predetermined idea of how the interplay should work—but that *both parties feel that they're respected partners in the gestation process leading to those work routines.*

It's best to *begin* with what I call the "After you, Alphonse" approach. You will certainly cross-pollinate where *ideas* are concerned, but where sheer *nuts and bolts* are concerned, respect the totality of your collaborator's domain; don't do any part of his job (even if only by way of giving "dummy" examples) until you're invited to participate . . . or until asking your partner if you might try something feels unforced, unobtrusive, and unthreatening. If there's sufficient trust and productivity, the line of demarcation will, in time, naturally soften and yield to a more natural, organic shape.

Yes, there are gray areas: neither composer nor lyricist can claim lyric scansion as exclusive birthright; lead-in dialogue going to song and internal dialogue *within* a song are likewise negotiable between lyricist and librettist. So *negotiate.* Remember the line Peter Stone wrote for cantankerous old Stephen Hopkins in *1776*: "In all my years I never heard, seen nor smelled an issue that was so dangerous it couldn't be *talked* about!"

Collaborations of three or more may not naturally lend themselves to a constant communal atmosphere. When *Gypsy* was being written, lyricist Stephen Sondheim was a creative intermediary much of the time. Knowing that conception, dramaturgy, and story structure were not composer Jule Styne's forte (that, indeed, Styne's thought process was a little too eccentric and volatile to be helpful when more reasoned analysis was called for), he would work with librettist Arthur Laurents separately. The two wordsmiths would deal with script issues, and then Sondheim would take those solutions to Styne, who required a different collaborative interplay, for development of the score. This is not an uncommon method of working: many composer/lyricist/librettist teams function according to a similar dynamic.

Nonetheless, the lines of communication have to remain open. It's okay for collaborators to work in discrete combinations. What's *not* okay is collaborative conspiracy, such as the lyricist and composer deciding that the librettist is a liability, and making an end run around him to the director. (If you examine the history of the shows whose development sustained serious creative team rifts or replacements, you'll find that *most* of them failed.) Disagreements must be aired openly, immediately, and—despite passions—reasonably . . . if not always coolly. Keep in mind, *you all want the same thing,* to make the show better. And keep in mind, too, that it is *just a show.* I don't mean to minimize what "a show" means to an artist—certainly mine mean a helluva lot to *me*—I mean merely to encourage a sense of perspective. Take deep breaths, stay rational, don't go crazy, and—very important—don't let the craziness of others rattle you. If only *one* person in a fierce disagreement remembers to keep a lid on his temper and keep the discussion focused, that's *usually* enough to get past the inevitable rough spots.

And when the rough spots do arise—*keep them confidential!* The inner workings of the primary creative team are *nobody else's business. Never* expose your disagreements, at least never in *any* way that lets *anyone* think that your interests and loyalties can be divided. If an opportunistic director, producer, or star senses that she can play one of you off against the other, she will, 85 percent of the time (a *very* conservative estimate). And then you might as well draw your own chalk outline and fit yourself for a toe tag. Because but for the lying down, you're already a corpse. And so's the show.

While most principles of collaboration can be filed under "standard procedure" with applicable variations, there is a more controversial, volatile scenario that must be mentioned, because it describes a reality most of us encounter, at one point or another.

What if you're in a collaboration that's yielding genuinely terrific work, but your collaborator, however artistically capable and diligent, is—let's put this diplomatically—emotionally problematic, beyond any hope of reform or interpersonal negotiation? If the difficult behavior primarily shows up *in private,* the answer depends entirely upon your stamina: assuming you can handle the angst, be philosophical about your partner's patterns, and honestly believe you can make it through the writing and production of an entire show (two to three years at a *minimum,* folks), then bear up as long as you can— and keep yourself open to other collaborations: you don't want to be joined at the hip to that kind of draining energy, not without some kind of relief or release. (This also includes having someone knowledgeable to talk to, because if you can't periodically vent, and be reassured that *you're* not the nutcase, you'll implode. Since venting necessitates a violation of confidentiality, choose your confessors and advisors *carefully.*) If, on the other hand, your partner's behavioral psychoses show up in *public* displays—and clearly demonstrate the potential to sabotage production opportunities and other relationships—then I would say cut your losses and run. *Once the environment becomes so poisonous that it seeps beyond collaborative controls, good work is almost never enough to compensate for bad reputations.* Many a promising voice has been marginalized or has vanished completely after exhausting industry patience.

Which brings us to . . .

MAINTENANCE (EXTERNAL)

Director Susan Schulman once told a group of BMI Workshoppers a story about her experience directing the vest-pocket revival of *Sweeney Todd.* Sondheim had been getting production notes from the producers, and in all cases, he advised them to express their concerns to the director. He confided in Schulman that this was a familiar tactic: producers approaching "the muscle" of a given production to make their influence felt; specifically, here, to sidestep the less politically powerful female director. But, Sondheim counseled her, long experience had taught him that *in production, a musical is the director's game,* insofar as the director *must* be perceived as the head of the operation, and *must* be the authority figure from which information is disseminated and to whom all must report; any other scenario would result in chaos. He assured Schulman that he would never endorse, condone, or cooperate with any effort to undermine her position. And he remained as good as his word.

Though this story isn't about collaborative writers, it is nonetheless a *flawless* model of collaborative etiquette. First and foremost, where "the outside world" is concerned, the members of a collaborative team *must* understand the importance of protecting each other. *Nothing* must be allowed to invade, or compromise the integrity of, the primary creative team.

Never let *anyone* in a position of power—director, producer, star, *anyone*—speak to you off the record or confidentially about your partner (at the very least, not about your partner's work on the project). If, for example, you're a lyricist, and you get a late-night phone call about the bookwriter's work, you can almost always bet the caller has already tried speaking to the bookwriter, or doesn't want to talk to the bookwriter directly, and is trying to make a detour past forthright communication. In such an instance, there are only two acceptable responses (including variations thereof): (1) "That's very interesting. But keep in mind, the libretto is my partner's bailiwick and it's ultimately his decision. I'll tell my collaborator what you said to me about his work, though"; or, even better: (2) "That's very interesting. I suggest you call my partner and tell him what you think." This cool, reasoned response, if adhered to assiduously, will always frustrate attempts to divide and conquer. It tells all would-be intruders, in no uncertain terms, that you and your collaborator(s) have no secrets from each other . . . and that anything said to one member of the team will be reported to the other(s). Don't let yourself be soft-soaped, flattered, bullied, or good-cop/bad-copped into behaving otherwise.

Sometimes, happily, you're not dealing with duplicity, but with a more open and honorable situation, such as a talking-heads session with other people on the production team. For example: I wrote two family audience shows for Theatreworks/USA. That company's artistic director at the time was its founder, Jay Harnick, who was famously, *obsessively* hands-on, and called regular meetings to assess every minute phase of a new show's development. If he asked me a question about a matter that I and my collaborator, librettist-director Rob Barron, were still trying to solve, I didn't have any problem saying to Jay, "I really can't discuss that right now. Rob and I need to deal with that in private first." And, to his credit, Jay always honored the boundary. Similarly, if it seemed that an objective opinion about an unresolved matter might be useful, I'd turn to Rob and ask: "Would you mind if I brought up what we were debating?" Rob is unusually even-handed, and would invariably say "Go ahead." But had he ever expressed ambivalence, I'd have backed off and tabled airing those views for another time. (It's perfectly fine to let a director or producer know—via cordial behavior—that you and your partner operate by a protocol that needs to be respected.) A truthful "We [or I] don't know the answer to that yet" is also a perfectly legitimate response that protects your privacy and your work process.

What if you're in a situation with a director or producer whose impatience, or whose natural energy, doesn't *allow* you to be as selectively guarded? In that case, take the time with your collaborator to discuss the method and motives of the person in question—and, based on that, devise your "second-best" strategies and/or protections. There will *always* be situations in which you'll have to improvise. Just try not to be flying blind when they arise.

ALWAYS ASK

A few principles:

Never give out any collaborative material (such as demos, scores, scripts) before clearing it with your partner(s).

Never make appointments, arrange meetings, schedule commitments, accept or refuse work, without consulting your partner(s). Similarly, never implement impulsive, eleventh-hour alterations to an understanding (for example—I know of a case where this actually happened—inviting producer X to a presentation that has been primarily assembled for the benefit of producer Y). You're in the game together. You *must* play like you're on the same team.

Never take an outside meeting that doesn't include your partner(s) unless express permission has been given, with complete understanding of how you are to represent the team's interests, and what the meeting is meant to accomplish.

Never assume your partner's agreement to, or refusal to accept, any set of working or presentation conditions (e.g., personnel, casting, locale). In many situations a collaborator will give you his/her proxy—often (but not always!) a librettist will trust the music department to cast a demo without her formal approval, for example—but remember that each collaboration is unique in this regard; don't assume that procedures taken for granted in one collaboration will perforce apply to another.

THE BUSINESS END

Don't do business . . . not with producers and not with each other (and don't be suckered by anyone who tells you differently)! *Business* is what agents and lawyers are for. (If you haven't got formal representation and money is a problem, the Dramatists Guild gives free legal counseling in certain contractual matters, and Volunteer Lawyers for the Arts should be able to advise and assist you on others.) Prior to getting a commitment for a production, finding a reliable agent to represent you can be something of a challenge . . . but once producers express interest, it only makes business sense for agents to be interested too. Whether one agent should represent the project as a whole or the collaborators should have individual agents is a judgment call. Assess the situation on its merits. If a collaborator wants separate representation, that's his right—don't make that a personal issue.

Surprisingly, despite fine points of negotiation, the basic formula governing immediate money issues is a no-brainer. Where expenses are concerned, each discipline (book, music, lyrics) is responsible for a third. This is true no matter how many people are on the primary creative team. Thus, if you are a composer-lyricist or lyricist-librettist, you cover two-thirds of any outgoing cost. What makes this fair is the fact that you *receive* two-thirds of the royalties when money starts coming *in,* because each discipline *nets* a third as well. Likewise, if there are two librettists, each is responsible for one-sixth of the expenses. The only expense that a team of two *should* split fifty-fifty—or that an oddly numbered team should divide evenly across the board—is the option fee for any property upon which they might base a musical. One school of thought favors dividing this cost per the royalty breakdown, too; but I advocate the even *per person* breakdown because in order for there to be legal and creative parity, all parties must control the underlying rights equally. (It's feasible that you might enter into a collaboration in which someone already controls an option on underlying rights—the producer, or a new collaborator—but then you may wish to have a representative negotiate your protections, since by definition the possibility exists that you can be removed from the project with no legal claim to "intellectual property" in the earnings from its future development.)

AND WHEN IN DOUBT . . .

. . . remember how it all started. With your intuition—your dating-savvy radar. Your antenna's functionality goes far beyond that first meeting. If a situation niggles at you, feels inherently unbalanced somehow—whether on your end, the end of a partner, or that of an outside influence—the chances are your instinct is right. Examine the situation, discuss it, don't be rash, and almost always you'll find a principle, just under the surface, that will guide you safely. Don't be intimidated by the complexities and subtleties you encounter, have faith in your moral and professional center . . .

   . . . and whenever possible, say it with flowers. . . .

2

CHAPTER

That Other Collaborator
or:
The Director

ONE OF THE BIGGEST, CONTINUING CHALLENGES OF YOUR career is partnering with a director who's right for the project—and for you.

Once you're into production of any sort—staged reading, workshop, full—your director is the leader, ever more so as the stakes and risks get higher. The director is the keeper, the *sharpener* of the vision, the disseminator of notes and news to the company, and ideally the protective buffer between you and the producers.

Ideally.

The director's leadership doesn't mean he controls the disposition of your material, nor that he can force you to make changes you'd rather not; that's where the Dramatists Guild—the professional association for theatre playwrights, composers, and lyricists—protects you (and if you're not a member, join, because sometimes the DG is *all* that protects you). But it's the director's job to keep the entire show in perspective and all its elements in balance.

Thus, when a director who's right for your project expresses concerns about the material and requests that something be rethought or revised or cut or differently organized or newly focused, he's to be taken *very* seriously. So it's vital that you work with a director whose input you can trust.

A phenomenon of the era of "star" and "concept" directors—such visionaries as Robbins, Fosse, Prince, Bennett—is that in their wake, *every* new director of any consequence fancies himself a conceptual auteur and sometimes even a real coauthor in the context of being the dramaturg who guides the writer(s) to and along the show's best path. And their agents try to negotiate for points accordingly.

Some directors have a genuine talent for this kind of hands-on direction.

Many (maybe even most) do not, but talk a great game; they can turn out to be ineffectual—or worse, damaging—as, at length, they pursue an agenda that conflicts with yours.

You have to be able to separate the ones who can deliver from the ones who won't, in order to protect yourself and your show.

It's not always easy.

The great talkers can have a certain facility for staging and visual execution, as well as prolific-enough careers to give them credibility; they'll ask the right questions, make sound observations at the start, give the impression that they're really on top of giving you what *you* want. And they can sound like kindred spirits: they've read the books, they know the anecdotes, they're conversant with the craft buzzwords and terms of art; and so just like the Devil, they can quote scripture to their own purposes. Paradoxically, they're not (usually) being insincere. Like most working artists, they believe what they *profess* to believe.

So you can't be swayed by intelligence alone, or even a decent-seeming track record (unless it's an *extreme* track record, like that of Hal Prince, or an absurdly persuasive one like that of Joe Mantello, who brilliantly brought home *Wicked* and the Broadway revival of *Assassins* in the same season).

What you're looking for, between the director and the authors, is a confluence of sensibility. A synergy. *Does the director have the vocabulary of the show in his or her arsenal?* The vocabulary includes: a basic feel for musical theatre language and conventions; emotional values; compatible taste in casting; affinity for needed style and thematic intent; visual sense; and understanding of the show's sociosexual dynamic. (And yes, I *do* mean, among other things, comfort with/empathy for gay vs. straight and male vs. female values. Never let *anyone* pressure you into believing this isn't a valid concern. The inappropriate sifting of material through filters that are variously homosexual, heterosexual, feminist, misogynistic, or otherwise potentially distortive is one of the most insidious dangers you'll encounter, not least because trying to address it directly is often fraught with personal, even political, peril—for doing so demands that the director be openly accountable for the imposition of a personal worldview and his private issues about intimacy.)

You have two ways to protect yourself. Avail yourself of both whenever possible.

THE FIRST PROTECTION

Follow your gut. Pay attention at that first meet-and-greet, not only to what the director says, but also to what he doesn't say. Note the aspects he emphasizes as opposed to those he doesn't. In early meetings, the wrong director will tend to give you *at least* one warning sign, if only subtly. The slightest derision of, disagreement with, eyebrow cocked at, something you find *essential* to your show is a clue to be taken *very* seriously—*even if the rest of the meeting goes swimmingly*. Never forget that of all the theatrical arts (with the exception of acting), directing is the most instinctive and impulsive. However thoroughly a director prepares, *half the job is done on the spot*, as he reacts to the various elements brought to bear and makes decisions as to how they're best combined. That's why those early-meeting clues are so important: because they, likewise, happen *reflexively*, and they're a polygraph-like barometer of the directoral instincts—and etiquette—at play. (Needless to say, if the director seems brilliant but untrustworthy as a human being, pay close heed to *that* impression too. Because if you approve him, you also green-light roundabout tactics that may not sit well with you.)

Here's a fairly obvious example of a warning sign: When Stephen Witkin and I were interviewing directors for our very first Rodgers Development Award staged reading of *The Fabulist*, our epic fable of Aesop, we were introduced to a young, talented fellow, known for directing large-cast Shakespeare productions, who kept talking about the physical presentation.

"You know," I said finally, "it's just a reading to test-run the material, see what we have."

He replied: "I know, I'm just very result oriented."

"Well . . . I think right now we're *process* oriented."

"Oh. Well, I've approached things from that direction, *too*. But story is not my forte, I usually work with a dramaturg."

We discussed things for several polite minutes more, but the meeting, for the authors, was already over.

Conversely, when we met with the insightful and energetic Sheryl Kaller, one of the things she said was, "I feel like Aesop's hunchback is sort of a physical metaphor, for the way he finds himself carrying the weight of the world." She was absolutely right—*and we'd never thought of it before.* As the meeting progressed, Stephen and I both had the strong, instinctive feeling that she not only "got" the play—she got *us*. And sure enough, when she directed the piece, it just *naturally* became much less scenically ambitious, less needful of a huge cast, more intimate, and much more humanist. And infinitely better.

Here's a much *subtler* example of a warning sign, the kind of thing I'm most concerned you're attuned to: when interviewing with a director for another musical, in a coffee shop with my collaborator and then-producer in tow, the director asked me to talk about the things in the show that excited me. At this point we were thirty minutes into the meeting and it seemed to be going great.

"Well," I said, "the subject matter suggests a kind of cinema verité realism in the performances—they're very real, earthy characters, but their passions are so big that they just *happen* to sing, naturally. I've never seen anything quite like that before and to me that's what makes the piece, in the best sense, theatrically dangerous."

And airily, the director said, "Oh, those verité musicals."

And I thought, *Uh oh.*

But the producer liked him, my collaborator liked him, hell, even *I* liked him, and *except for that one blip*, the rest of the meeting was swell, so we went ahead.

And sure enough the verité humanism I found so essential to the piece *was the first thing he began to chip away at.* We worked with the fellow for a year, the deterioration to the show in general started to spiral out absurdly, and, to oversimplify a complex story, I pulled the plug, wishing like hell I had trusted my antenna at the start.

There is a happy ending. Two years later the project was resurrected— with an appropriate director at the helm.

But the year with the wrong guy is a year I'll never get back.

THE SECOND PROTECTION

The second way to protect yourself is to see as many productions as possible that your potential director has helmed. These days, with electronic documentation so pervasive, you needn't worry about having missed anything live. The director's most significant work has probably been preserved on videotape or digitally. (New York City dwellers and visitors can even do research unannounced; the video archives at the Lincoln Center Library for the Performing Arts are very comprehensive; most tech-age productions of any consequence are routinely preserved there for posterity, including regional ones—some dating back as far as 1970.) If the approach of the director includes what you're looking for, the chances are decent to excellent that the match will be a good one. If the work does *not* show what you're looking for, then the match will not be good. Just as your written work makes the most eloquent case for *your* ability, an actual production says more for a *director's* suitability than *any* conversation.

AND ONCE ACTUAL COLLABORATION BEGINS . . .

. . . be careful not to *over*react to a *good* director's "interference" and influence. There is *always* a period of trial and error, of setting territories, boundaries, limitations, freedoms. You have to allow time for the comfort/trust zone to develop. Even in the best and happiest of environments, it never appears fully formed at the start; it has to evolve around the interacting idiosyncrasies of the players. Peter Stone once remarked that it's okay for a writer exploring a new relationship to be at the director's shoulder, giving constant notes and expressing the minutest concerns—up until the point where (as he put it), the director says, "Get the hell away from me!" After that, Stone continued, you need to be more temperate and select your battles more carefully; but his assertion was that unless you go that far once—and *only* once—you never know how far you *can* go. There are less overt ways of pushing this envelope, too, but Stone describes a common-enough scenario, which produces information that's important to know.

Understand too that most directors are by nature at least *somewhat* manipulative; it's implicit in the job description and that need to be in charge is a primary factor in what attracts them to the profession in the first place. So you need to perceive the difference between "constructive manipulation" that urges you toward your best work (much as it urges actors toward deeper performances), which can represent a gifted director at his most resourceful—and "power manipulation." The latter tries to suppress or manage the input of a strong-minded or less experienced author, and comes in various forms: passive-aggressive avoidance of phone calls and emails; the obvious outright pissing contest; or something as subtle as the unspoken implication that if you don't do things the director's way, she'll bolt, which, when producers are involved, can be a political hot button (and you can bet the director knows it and counts on your fear of pushing it).

At some point, too, you and your director will argue, or debate, passionately over aspects of the show. How the director argues is very telling. There's nothing to fear in a vigorous, lively exchange of ideas, toward a mutually satisfactory answer. (And always remember: oftentimes the answer is neither A nor B—but C. Knowing and acknowledging this out loud usually liberates debate from the shackles of anger, anxiousness, and ego.) Even if the director becomes insistent, so long as you're confident that he's looking out for the show's best interests, there's no harm in examining the issue from the other side.

But beware any attempt to cast you in the role of newbie (even if you *are* a newbie), or to infantilize you by trying to make a weapon out of a brief resume, youth, inexperience, or *different* experience. (One team of writers I know, who had carved out a career writing numerous young-audience musicals, suffered the indignity of a producer and director trying to steer their show in a questionable direction, telling them, "You need to understand you're in the big leagues now. This is a Broadway-bound musical, it's not like writing for Theatreworks/USA." The condescension of this remark aside, it's also bullshit, and speaks to the ignorance, arrogance, and manipulativeness of the power brokers on this project: There is no *better* training ground for the aspiring professional than a Theatreworks/USA musical, nor a development process closer to what you'll encounter in first-class venues, nor a more demanding audience than kids. And any director or producer worth dealing with *knows* that.)

Beware too the director who instigates or (in league with a producer) forces you into a creative meeting immediately after a performance, especially an evening performance. This is the *worst* time to discuss *anything;* nobody has perspective, often one or more of the participants is fried, nerves are frayed, and stamina is waning. Harold Prince has it as an inviolate principle that after an evening performance, the creative team is to go home and get a night's sleep, so that problems can be approached freshly and energetically the next day. (That said, there are circumstances in which immediate postperformance meetings are necessary, but context, the goodwill of your colleagues, and your own common sense will make those plain.)

Finally, beware of sexual or, more commonly, social harassment or blithe disregard for your basic human sensitivity. The generous director will try, as much as possible, to protect you from spirit-diminishing forces; and will guide you past any genuine naïveté caringly—if not always gently—and with appreciation for your strengths, since your strengths are, presumably, why he wanted to work with you to begin with.

Ultimately, you know when you and your artistic intentions are being treated with respect, and when they're not. The directors whose chronically abusive behavior is worth putting up with for the sake of the end result are few and far between.

THE FINAL CAUTION

If you find, in the early days, or at the conclusion of a developmental step (say, a reading), that you've made a mistake in approving a new director, it's okay to withdraw that approval. Do it as professionally, forthrightly, honestly, and cleanly as you can. But don't hesitate. If things are dicey, they will *only* get worse unless you act decisively.

The hardest thing to do in this business—because we're all so hungry for opportunity—is to say NO to, or put the brakes on, a bad circumstance in the face or promise of forward movement. But remember: in the long run, you will *never* be sorry you said no; because it always gives you the later chance to reexamine the material in a healthy environment. However, you will *always* regret saying YES to something you don't believe in. Aside from the bitterness, frustration, and (often) lack of psychological closure it leads to, it also—on a purely pragmatic level—shuts doors. Once material has been exposed in a harmful light, or "overshopped" with the wrong people at the helm, it becomes infinitely harder, and at times impossible, to resurrect it free of its former taint.

But oh, for the YES that rings true. . . .

3
CHAPTER

The Guards and the Suits
or:
Agents and Producers

HOW YOU GET THEM

THE BAD NEWS UP TOP. THERE'S NO SILVER BULLET, NO guaranteed method, for getting agents and producers interested in you. There are time-tested procedures that adjust to prevailing trends as the industry changes, but the process is now, as it ever was, a combination of perseverance, talent, and luck. And getting produced these days involves a greater proportion of luck than ever. The good news is, I don't know any writer who deserved representation who was unable to find an agent eventually.

These days, with showcases, workshops, readings, and the like, it's very common for an agent or producer to respond to material in a performance event she's been invited to. The winning of a prestigious musical theatre award for aspiring musical dramatists and/or their shows (e.g., the Kleban, the Rodgers, the Larson, the Gilman & Gonzlez-Falla) also draws attention and tends to rate extra consideration.

Submit scripts and demos according to guidelines set forth by the agent or producer, or standard protocols (see the section "You Are What You Submit" later in this book). (Every year, the Dramatists Guild publishes a newly revised directory of agents and producers. Get it and work your way through it.) It's also not bad to know somebody who can make a personal recommendation.

AGENTS

An agent, like a collaborator, is a professional with whom you need to have a comfortable working relationship. In the strictest sense, your agent works for you (taking a 10–15 percent commission from your earnings), but I've never encountered an agent who behaved like a client's employee. An agent should be regarded as a white-collar professional whose expertise, advice, counsel, and *protection* you seek as you would that of a lawyer or doctor. You want both competence and a sense of symbiosis—that she has the sensitivity and smarts to respond to your needs and nurture your strengths while you have the industry and talent to provide her with enough ammo to work on your behalf.

If you feel an agent is condescending, distant, or chronically unavailable, this is not a good, normal sign. If you feel a particular agent, though able, simply isn't a good personal fit—or seems too languid to be an aggressive negotiator, or too volatile to be politically appropriate—that also is to be considered seriously.

On those occasions when you're *just not sure,* and want to wait out the relationship and see how things feel over time . . . this too is legitimate (especially if the agent's client list includes impressive names; you like to think you're in good company for a reason). But don't wait too long. If you have a backlog of viable work, six months to a year is plenty. If you're too deeply into development or creation to have provided your agent with product to represent, you may need to be more lenient with him and tougher on yourself.

Your agent should be someone discreet, savvy, resourceful, creative about deal-making, and connected, in whom you can confide comfortably, and on whom you can depend for professional protection and advice—without fear of exposing your personal mishegoss, because there is a unique kind of intimacy in the agent-client relationship, and his knowing what makes you tick is among his primary tools.

Okay, let's say you've *got* an agent. And one you feel good about. Let's debunk a fallacy first. Unless you attain the kind of "stardom" or high-profile success that allows them to field offers, *agents don't get you work.* This is not to say they can't facilitate a connection, submit you for an open project, or make a recommendation that leads somewhere. If your agent is a good one, certainly he will try. But in general, it is up to you to generate your own work, and give your agent something to sell to the buyers. That's simply the nature of the biz.

What you can expect a good agent to do is this:

- **Send out script and demo packages that are ready for consideration, to producers and institutional theatres likely to produce it (according to its size and sensibility).** You and your agent should decide on this list together.

- **Follow up on those submissions in a reasonably timely manner and relay the feedback, positive or negative, to you.** Positive feedback speaks for itself, especially if it denotes interest or an offer. Negative feedback can be selectively dismissed, but consider if it does point to a needed revision that might make the piece stronger for future submissions elsewhere.

- **Negotiate the deal that best protects your financial interests,** the various rights involved (box-office royalties, publishing, recording, mechanicals, stock and amateur licensing, etc.)—and your professional treatment.

- **Negotiate the deal that best protects the integrity and the copyright of your work.** The Dramatists Guild contract is the Kevlar vest that says no one can make changes to your work without your permission or participation; but due to certain clauses, there are ways to vary it, and your agent should be able to vary it in your favor. Plus, some institutional theatres and production outfits refuse to follow the DG template, generating their own contracts, and your agent must know how to amend those so that they're DG-equivalent where it matters. In most theatrical contexts, producers don't buy your work outright, they lease it for a finite period of time, which is commensurate with your DG protections—but there are other contexts, such as film and television, where this may not be so. In these cases your agent needs to negotiate for the compensating perks (above all money) that go along with you and your work being treated more like alterable, disposable commodities.

- **Keep you apprised of work being done on your behalf on a regular basis.** Which speaks for itself. Note that if you're not actively generating work, you'll receive less frequent bulletins.

- **Be the buffer between you and ANYTHING concerning business.** It's your agent's job to be the "heavy," where negotiation is concerned. That way you don't *have* to be. Ideally you should *never* be involved in talking business whatsoever, though I have to admit, even the most resourceful agent is only a human being, and if someone on the other side is stonewalling, there are circumstances (and it's a judgment call every time) in which you may *have* to insert yourself into the process just to get enough data to help your agent keep moving things along. But in general *these are extreme cases and unusual in their particulars.*

- **Advise you on politics and procedure.** Along with negotiating your deals, this is perhaps the most important function your agent has, and one of which you should take full advantage. Your agent can help you strategize a meeting with an important new contact; can talk you down off the ceiling toward a rational response when you're upset by a difficult or frustrating situation; can vet an important letter or email before you send it, to ensure that not only the content, but also the *tone* is correct; can express concern or even indignation *on your behalf* when to do so yourself is politically dicey; can advise you about the viability of one project over another; can help you prioritize deadlines; can simply be a general, professional sounding board about people, projects—and yourself.

Caution

Agents are in the selling and deal-making business—and they enjoy a mark in the WIN column as much as anyone. In both my own experience and the experience of others, breaks are so hard to come by that usually only when the danger signs are overt, or suspected via prior experience, will an agent say of a definite offer, "The money is real, but you're going to be miserable. Let's hang tight and see if we can't do better." There will be times when, even as your agent is eager to close a deal, your belly says, *This feels wrong,* or *I don't like/trust this producer as a person.* You should *never* ignore those sensations! Your antenna is sending you a true signal. If your agent is a good one she may well try to talk you out of it, but in the end, if you follow your heart, and your heart still tells you something's amiss, a good agent should always be willing to respect your feelings and your wishes without consequence to your personal or working relationship.

PRODUCERS

Where producers are concerned, I've had experiences that run the gamut from lovely, to middling, to the-Treasury-Department-hasn't-printed-the-money-that-would-get-me-to-do-it-again. However, because I am careful to apply previous experience to potential new experiences, I haven't had a bad producer in a very long time. Some were "imperfect" in ways I had to make peace with. And I had one, maybe two, narrow escapes, where I called a halt prior to any legal or implied ethical commitment. But I've had none since "enlightenment" that I've regretted. And based on that, I *can* tell you this much:

Once you've been burned by a producer, there's no point in repeating the experience . . .

. . . once you find a producer is well-intentioned but unable to deliver, there's no point in holding onto false hope, and you should start thinking of how you'll move on . . .

. . . and once you find a producer with whom you have a functional relationship—*cultivate it!*

Even if the producer has maddening idiosyncrasies or procedures (such as hands-on project-nursing so obsessive-compulsive as to be stifling, or so laid-back a style that *you* have to follow up on every detail to be sure everything gets done properly), should the end result be that you're getting your work supported and/or produced and/or exposed on a continuing basis, in a way and venue that you can take pride in, don't rock the boat without *unassailable* reason.

(A small but important amendment to the "once burned" advisory: It applies much more rigidly to individuals in the commercial arena than to organized, prolific offices and not-for-profit institutional or regional venues. When you're dealing with a full-fledged production outfit that pumps out multiple productions per season, you're also dealing with the shifting variables and multiple personalities of a corporate hierarchy, whose procedures—if they're industry survivalists—necessarily become adjusted and refined with experience and changing trends; in such an instance, it may be worth examining how much the environment has changed since your last experience, or how thoroughly they learned from their mistakes right along *with* you. If the stronger consideration is the relationship with a viable organization, cultivating that relationship may still be the answer, because you're looking beyond a single project to a potential long haul.)

There are too many variables where producers are concerned to make comprehensive, sweeping statements. With consortium producers, independent producers, regional producers, visionary producers, dilettante producers, institutional producers, vanity producers, and add-the-adjective-of-your-choice, every situation has the potential to be unique. And you can't apply the same comfort-zone standards to a producer that you would to a collaborator or an agent. David Merrick, for example, was just as famous for his tantrums, his attempts (successful and un-) to interfere, his penchant for divide-and-conquer tactics, and his ruthlessness as he was for his passion and resourcefulness. But no one would deny his track record or viability as a player.

So where producers are concerned, issues of trust and respect may not always be *wholly* accurate barometers. You may find yourself examining the *type,* the *degree,* or the *regularity* of questionable behavior before drawing the right conclusion. The nicest producers may prove unable to deliver, the ones who seem arrogant tyrants may have the muscle, faith, and conviction you need at your back.

Therefore, **your best preparation is homework:** Investigate the producer's production history, find out who he has worked with before, ask questions of other artists who've been on the firing line when the producer was getting *their* shows into production. (When tracking production history, the Internet Broadway Database [www.ibdb.com] and the Internet Off-Broadway Database [www.iobdb.com or www.lortel.org/LLA_archive/index.cfm] are invaluable sources to start with.)

If the producer has been involved with successes—how? As a money provider? Or hands on? Has he ever been hands on before? How did *those* shows turn out? What did people on *those* productions think?

If the producer is an old-schooler: How recently has he been active? When he was active, what kind of projects was he involved with? Do the answers that are emerging indicate he still has the wherewithal to raise enough capital to bring a show in?

If the producer is younger, is her primary specialty something other than producing—say, general managing or marketing—and is she trying to break in? Has she gotten anything off the ground before? New production or transfer? Hands-on development or administrative facilitator?

If the producer is an institutional or regional theatre, have they done musicals before (and did they know what they were doing)? If they haven't, are they versatile and resourceful enough to make a thorough go of it?

What can you find out about productions the producer started to develop—and then parted company with?

When answers emerge that are controversial, try your discreet best to get the story from all sides. As you do, never underestimate the ability of someone who feels wounded, rejected, or disempowered by a bad situation to shift and edit the weight of remembered words and events to create a tale in which they are painted as the righteous party. And be charitable, for egos in this business can be more fragile than they appear, and often this revisionism is borne of a subconscious defense mechanism in which the fiction has become the perceived truth, not a deliberate camouflage or prevarication. Reinvented history is an occupational hazard and you must constantly, *tacitly*, be attuned to the possibility of it (even within yourself). Parties involved whose careers were *not* at stake—actors, musical directors, stage managers, rehearsal pianists, etc.—are often excellent, relatively objective sources.

Also consider if the producer has an affinity for your kind of show. Even if the producer expresses enough interest to take an option, you want to be certain he's interested in it for the same reasons you are. I cannot *tell* you the number of times I've heard of one producer or another optioning an adventurous piece, and then campaigning to make the piece less adventurous, for fear the "marketplace" will reject the very thing that makes the show attractive in the first place. Often the right director can navigate through this situation and protect you, but how early he comes on board, and whether his allegiance is *to the show* or *to the producer* is a key factor.

Finally, there is a recent trend for producers to agree to produce your show *contingent upon their being allowed to direct it.* This can be an advantage, a devil's bargain, or both. Can the producer direct at all? Has she directed successfully before? Does she have a workable musical theatre reflex in her arsenal? Is she hip enough to learn from you, and from appreciation of the form, what she doesn't know yet from hands-on experience? Is this a compromise, and if so, one you can live with? What long-term gain to your career, and what possible risk to your show? All these questions have to be considered

very

very

carefully
thoughtfully
and
thoroughly.

As I say: with producers you can't hew to rules, rules will flummox you.

What likely will not flummox you is your gut.

In my feckless youth, I was at an opening-night party. I had a passing acquaintance with one of the producers, a very effective professional, but one whose admirable candor could be expressed at times with stunning insensitivity—call him Phil. He greeted me effusively and asked what I was working on. I mentioned a property he liked, and he smiled hugely. Then he asked who the producer was. I mentioned the name—let's say Donny. Phil's smile vanished fast, he made a face of brusque distaste, and said: "Donny's not a real producer." Whereupon he immediately turned to other people and I found myself very mad. I took a few deep breaths and thought, *You know what Phil is like, why let it upset you?* But it was not a rhetorical question. I really wondered why I was so upset. And I finally answered myself thus: *Because, in his gruff, bite-me way, he just told you what you were already afraid of.* When Phil disengaged himself from the other people, I took a deep, brave breath and said, "Man, you can't just say that about Donny without tellin' me why. Why is he not a real producer?" And Phil candidly discussed attitude, track record, expertise, and a few personal encounters—as only a real producer could—and even told a story in which Donny tried to partner with Phil on a project, and Phil rejected the overture. Each bit of data confirmed a feeling I had tried to ignore. Sure enough, within a few months, my agent decided to part company with Donny. Happily, it was a friendly parting—no papers had been signed, it had all been handshakes and smiles up until then—which makes this a fairly benign story. But I know lots worse stories I *can't* tell, where other writers' rights and trust were virtually *raped* by producers they felt funny about *right at the start,* and many thousands of unhappy dollars were subsequently spent by the writers in buyouts and legal fees to get their shows clear—if they could.

On the other hand, the composer-lyricist team of Robert Lopez and Jeff Marx have had an amazing, even meteoric success with *Avenue Q.* They have even publicly admitted that they made a number of important compromises along the way, some of which involved a significant degree of soul-searching. But they knew they were in good hands and on a good ride (with, among others, the Vineyard Theatre and The New Group as coproducers), they correctly sensed it would take them where they wanted to go, and they made their decisions intelligently, by trusting their hearts—along with their trusted advisors.

Go back to the end of the previous chapter on directors and reread "The Final Caution" because it's just as true here: Compromise when you can, but NEVER say *yes* when your belly says *no*. Don't rush to take the first offer that comes your way. If the offer is sincere, you'll have ample time to think it over. And if your show is good enough, and complete enough, there will be others. Eventually.

The hardest part after NO is the waiting. But you can do it.

Let your YES be a source of joy.

4

C H A P T E R

Throwing "The Book" at You
or:
The Plainly Visible Secrets of Successful Libretti

BECAUSE THE MUSICAL LIBRETTO IS OFTEN *MISPERCEIVED* AS A work of "mere" prose, and therefore the product of a less precise discipline, it has taken on an aura of false mystery. It is said (correctly, for the most part), that no matter how good a score may be, if the book doesn't work, the show doesn't work. Yet book basics are the least well-understood part of the craft, and the least well-dealt-with in print analyses of musical theatre as an art form, and that contributes to why so many shows fail, often needlessly.

Paradoxically, the basics are there for all who know the classic literature; they're hiding in plain sight—craft principles just as immutable as those regarding the use of perfect rhyme and graspable melodic shape.

You can reject these principles—selectively—*as and if you choose to experiment with form.* But you should *know* them, *think* about them, and *understand the risks* of putting them aside.

KA-CHING—THE MAGIC TEN

Let's talk about what I will cautiously call "the selling points" first.

I say "cautiously" because you can't write for a "marketplace" in the musical theatre. You can only write the things you care about passionately in the most honest way you can. If you try to second-guess, or bend to, some perceived marketplace, your show will betray your mercenary intentions and fail. Every time. The marketplace—a term that *does*, sometimes regrettably, inform film, records, and television—moves too quickly for a developing musical to *ever* keep pace with it. A developing musical may *coincidentally anticipate* a marketplace trend (or, like *Hair,* exist as part of a cultural phenomenon), but that's a circumstance borne strictly of unpredictable timing. Save for Maury Yeston and Peter Stone's *Titanic,* which approximately coincided with the release of James Cameron's film, I can't think of a musical that managed the trick. You can't manufacture it, so don't even try.

Indeed, that's why there are "eternal verities" (a.k.a. common selling points) in the construction of most successful musicals. Since the musical is a form that *cannot* be fitted to a prevailing, temporary wave, it must therefore bow to the features that have been time-tested for, at this writing, over sixty years. In the tradition of all the best lists, there are ten of them.

Here's the big starter. Can't stress it enough.

Selling Point #1: A larger-than-life, or at the very least, hugely *passionate*, and *active* hero or heroine with a *hugely ambitious objective* that can be interpreted as his or her quest. That hero and the hero's quest are what drive the show. Does this sound like part of a by-the-numbers formula? It's not. It is, in fact, a template, upon which *many* a variation has succeeded. Check it out:

- In *1776,* John Adams, a fiery congressman, wants American independence.
- In *Man of La Mancha,* Don Quixote, an addled old man who fancies himself a knight-errant, wants to bring nobility and decency back to a base and debauched world.
- In *Sweeney Todd: The Demon Barber of Fleet Street,* the title character wants revenge upon the judge and the corrupt system that destroyed his life and his family.
- In *Gypsy,* Mama Rose, the ultimate stage mother, wants to achieve the success *she* never could attain in show business by getting it vicariously, through her kids.
- In *Fiddler on the Roof,* Tevye, a proudly patriarchal milkman ("I have five daughters!") in a small Russian village at the turn of the twentieth century, tries desperately to hold onto old-world tradi-

tions and values in a world where traditions and values are inexorably changing.

- In *How to Succeed in Business Without Really Trying,* J. Pierpont Finch wants to climb the corporate ladder in a few easy steps.
- In *The Producers,* Max Bialystock, a down-on-his-luck Broadway producer, decides to reverse his fortunes by putting on "the worst play ever written," and absconding with the money he raises to back it (millions more than it would require) on the premise that no one checks the books on a bomb.
- In *Hairspray,* set in 1962, overweight but adorable teen Tracy Turnblad dreams of being famous *and* integrating the local *American Bandstand*–like *Corny Collins* TV show, so that black artists and dancers appear not just on Negro Day—but *every* day!
- In *The King and I,* British schoolteacher Anna Leonowens seeks no less than to be a civilizing influence on the king of Siam, for the benefit it will do his people.

Now—*why* is this so important?

Musicalizing a story intensifies it. A passionate character on a quest fits naturally into an intense universe, a larger-than-life character even more so. The character complements the intention (as well as the intensity) of the form.

Now, *larger-than-life* is a fairly liberal term. Strictly speaking, *How To's* Finch and *Hairspray's* Tracy start off as unremarkable civilians—*but only insofar as they are perceived by most of the rest of their world.* To us, however, they are *wholly* remarkable because their desire to achieve greatness means they are misfits in a normal world. What distinguishes Finch is his brazen self-centeredness; and what distinguishes Tracy is her *apparent* (but deceptive) unsuitability for the kind of popularity she desires: *in 1962 it just didn't happen to fat girls.*

By the same token, prosaic characters with everyday wants are *horrid* choices for musicalization; being prosaic, they work against the natural emphasis of the form. They simply aren't strong or memorable or resonant enough to drive a musical, *in most cases.*

Also avoid passive main characters who are observers or ciphers, because their natural stance is to *avoid* action as they absorb information. A different kind of passivity—just as unfriendly to musicalization—is exhibited by the character who is acted *upon.* (The recent Broadway musical of *Jane Eyre* was destined to fail no matter *how* well it might have been executed, because the title character does not drive the story, and thus the narrative lacks a central, forward-moving energy. Her inner life may be one of turbulence, but as long as she avoids taking matters into her own hands, she exists in a state of suspended animation. Film can handle this kind of psychological profiling; it is anathema to musicals.)[1]

Finally, the denouement must occur as a result of action taken by the main character. Just as he or she powers the story, he or she must also be responsible for its conclusion. That doesn't mean a supporting character can't *react* to a situation *set up* by the main character and push the goal over the top (sometimes the main character is on a quest that requires some ultimate approval by another); but you should never employ *deus ex machina*, an ending that is not a direct result of your lead's design and ambition.

Selling Point #2: Interesting and functional supporting characters. Supporting characters should also be idiosyncratic. Each one of any consequence, however minor, should have a trait, a quirk of personality, a desire, *something* that immediately sets him or her apart. And of course, the less archetypal the characters, the more profoundly you should highlight their distinctiveness. Even a character performing an archetypal *function* should have an unconventional *spin*. (If you can anchor this idiosyncrasy to the storytelling, theme, and/or structure . . . better still. That kind of layering and interconnectedness is what helps give a musical depth, substance, and weight, so that even the lightest of them speak resonantly to the human condition.)

More than this, though, supporting characters need to have a primary connection to the main plot and the main character. There are indeed a number of classic musicals from the forties through the

---

1. A famous anomaly is Bobby in *Company*. For the most part he observes the married couples who are his "good and crazy" friends. But in a structural sense, *Company* is a revue of sketches with songs, supporting a superimposed story (George Furth's libretto originally started out as five one-act plays about marriage; Bobby was later created as a linking device). Although the show survives in the canon, it pays to note that actors find Bobby notoriously difficult to "make their own," because he's so ill-defined at the core, making major transitions without sufficiently defined motivation; and that, while the score by Stephen Sondheim remains fresh and dynamic, the book has not aged well at all. Its stylistic innovations are still felt today—which is why its star of repute has never faded—but those once-potent sketches are now sitcom standard, and revivals of the show are less and less frequent.

mid-sixties in which secondary characters propel what TV writers call B-stories—stories that run *parallel* to the A-story without significantly *impacting* it—but, as screenwriter-novelist William Goldman has noted[2]: in the intervening decades *storytelling has changed*. It's a lot tighter and a lot less leisurely these days; it's also more sophisticated, packed and consolidated. Audiences grasp *more* things in *less* time and become increasingly intolerant of repetition or sidebars. The era of Ado Annie and Will Parker as "comic relief" for Curly and Laurie (*Oklahoma!*) is gone. These days, look toward Anthony and Johanna (*Sweeney Todd*)—their story *cannot exist* without Sweeney's, *nor can it end without returning to him;* John Dickinson (*1776*) would not trouble himself to rally the conservatives in Congress unless John Adams were a threat to their status quo. *Even when the lead is not onstage, the remaining characters must play out the applicable reverberations of his or her actions.* (Can you sing "If Mama Was Married"?)

All this talk about the *kinds* of characters that best populate a musical leads us inevitably to the third principle.

Selling Point #3: A story that is character driven, not plot driven. This does not mean musicals aren't plotted. Some, like *Sweeney Todd* and *1776* are *highly* plotted. But the plot doesn't fuel the proceedings. Your main character must actively *make* the story happen through his/her desires and actions.

And the completion (or frustration!) of the lead's quest usually represents some kind of transformation or rite of passage. Your main character will rarely end up the same person s/he began.

This is why genre material tends to work against musicalization. Science fiction, mystery, action-adventure, and so on tend to be about the pursuit of knowledge, the correction of an injustice, the exploration of an idea, the battle between unchanging forces of good and evil, and the like.[3]

In an average episode of *Columbo*, for example, the good lieutenant in

---

2. In the foreword to his screenplay for *Maverick*, in *Five Screenplays with Essays* (ApplauseBooks).

3. If this sounds an ironic precept to come from a fellow who coauthored a serious-minded science fiction musical, bear in mind, the stories upon which the two one-acts in *Weird Romance* are based only utilize science-fiction milieux. The main characters go through profound personal growth, and indeed the stories were selected because in each, the main character *embodies* the idea being explored. This confluence of elements in a genre story—much less one that lends itself to musicalization—is very rare.

the rumpled raincoat comes into the story late, *after* the murder has been committed. Now, a *Columbo* episode is certainly about character, as almost every installment is a "closed" rather than "open" mystery (we know who committed the crime from the start), and the thing we delight in is the game of cat-and-mouse he plays with the killer. *But the situation is already in motion when Columbo arrives—he* hasn't created it, the *killer* has—nor is he meaningfully transformed by the outcome of events. As a main character, he's attractive because he's a *constant,* and *how he'll solve the puzzle* is what drives the story; not who he is and what he has personally at stake. (More on this in the chapter on adaptation.)

Selling Point #4: Conflict that kicks in early and doesn't resolve until the end. Your main character wants something, and that need puts him or her at odds with powerful forces opposed to the goal.

Don't wait to introduce this. As soon as your main character sings her "I Want" or defining "I Am" song, start bringing on the odds she'll be working against—if you haven't done so already.

Keep the quest alive, and increase the jeopardy.

There can be moments of celebration and achievement along the way, but the tension should not release until the denouement. Never give main characters the excuse to be complacent, save as a momentary device to ratchet up the tension later.

Put more simplistically, don't let them express happiness unless you can pull the rug out from under them right after—until the end of the show. An example: the act break of *Fiddler on the Roof,* when the Cossacks disrupt the wedding.

How do you maintain this story tension in an organized fashion?

There have been entire books and several lauded days-long symposia devoted to story structure, and it would be absurd of me to try and cover all the fine points here (my recommended reading list is in Appendix III at the back of this book); but the traditional three-act structure that informs screenwriting and well-made playwriting tends to inform most enduring musicals as well. The word "acts" in *this* context, by the way, is defined by turning points in the story, not the placement of the intermission. In fact, let's call them "structure acts" to avoid confusion.

Structure Act One is the exposition that sets up your characters, conflicts, and story. (George M. Cohan: "In Act One, get your man up a tree.")

Structure Act Two escalates the main character's quest and the challenges to it, until s/he reaches a point of no return, a place of jeopardy, risk, impending disaster, and/or choice where his/her life can never be what it was before. In a traditional musical, the intermission tends to be placed at this act's end. (Cohan: "In Act Two, throw stones at him.")

Structure Act Three chronicles the character's efforts to meet the big challenge and how they lead to "endgame" and resolution. (Cohan: "In Act Three, get him out of the tree.")

Since musicals, despite all these libretto principles, invite stylistic and presentational experimentation, the three-act structure is arguably the element to be applied least rigidly. But study as many classic musical libretti as you can. Note how the stories peak, build, pause for intermission (if they do), and resolve—you'll note that in most instances, the exceptions are not really breaks with tradition, but subtle variations borne of specific context and content. In the craft of musical storytelling, ultimately, as with any good writing, form follows function and content dictates style.

That said, here's a short list of things that are the enemy of narrative tension:

- dramatic passivity
- inexact focus
- lack of overall objective
- moments in which the main story points are dropped or lost

A great and frequent technique for avoiding the enemy is the creation of what's called "the ticking clock"—a time limit on the hero's objective that gives it urgency. John Adams has to push the Declaration of Independence through by July 4. Sweeney Todd has to finally exact his revenge upon Judge Turpin before Anthony can spirit Johanna away. In *Her Pilgrim Soul*, act two of my own *Weird Romance,* Nola, a spectral visitor from the turn of the twentieth century, seemingly reincarnated in a high-tech lab's hologram chamber, is remembering/reliving her life at the rate of ten years per day. The scientist Kevin must discover why she's there before that life is over.

The opening gambit as described (main character enters, sings "I Want," is confronted by obstacles) is the classic execution, but there are variant configurations that can also work, depending, per above, upon what content and function require. In *1776,* for example, John Adams delivers the first spoken words of the show right after the overture, expressing his desire for American independence *before* he sings. *Then* the show curtain flies up so the Congress can try to shush him with "Sit Down, John"—and after *that,* since we already *know* what he wants, he expands upon his frustration, in a complaint that is a cagily indirect "I Am" song ("Piddle, Twiddle and Resolve") that also fills us in on what he considers the maddening, cautious routines of the Continental Congress. And that rage segues into the more tender "Yours, Yours, Yours," which allows the authors to introduce the convention of the dramatized letters between Adams and his wife Abigail (who tries to both placate him and make sure he stays cognizant of problems *outside* of Philadelphia). The crucial thing to note here is that the span from Adams' first monologue through "Yours, Yours, Yours" *describes the opening sequence of the show. The momentum is continuous throughout and the musical does not stop for applause until the ground rules for the evening are established!*

Which leads us to—

Selling Point #5: The set-up of what are called your "permissions"— your dramatic theme, your stylistic conceits, your tone, your vocabulary, your ground rules—right at the top. And then sticking to them. Little is deadlier to a musical than a delay in the audience getting its bearings. I once heard John Guare offer a class this principle of playwriting: "The audience gives a playwright fifteen to twenty minutes to fuck around. After that, if he doesn't have them, he's lost them forever." I've been a drama critic for three decades, and that's a fairly accurate blanket assessment.

Here's the bad news:

You don't have anywhere *near* that much time with a musical.

A play allows for a more leisurely introduction of elements because it tends to open with exposition and character introduction through dialogue. However theatricalized the style, this reflects a naturalistic rhythm, an emulation of real time.

A musical, however, opens with a *number.* As close to the top as possible. A number with some mood-setting, energy-creating muscle behind it. This makes a big, bold, self-assured statement—and its forthrightness, its compactness, its confidence implies a promise that the creators know *exactly* what they're about. The number can transmit a certain amount of exposition, and often does—but the story is usually set in earnest motion in the moments *after.* The opening number makes a pact with the audience. A pact delivered in theatrical *shorthand.* It's a different language, and audience expectation adjusts accordingly. And with this expectation come the permissions—the ones your opening moment asks the audience to give you: permission to be funny, to be thrilling, to be moving, to be epic, to be highly choreographed, and so on. It's a permission that works in reverse as well. Perhaps the most famous story illustrating this point is the one about how *A Funny Thing Happened on the Way to the Forum* nearly closed out of town because it had the wrong opening number, a charming tune called "Love Is in the Air" that left the audience baffled. The subsequent "Comedy Tonight" gave the audience *permission to laugh and to expect a farce.*

Furthermore, as an audience adjusts to the style, tone, and expectation of implied or specified theatrical devices, they also adjust to dramatic theme. Which reminds me:

Selling Point #6: An underlying dramatic theme. One way or another, every good musical—profoundly or lightheartedly—is about *something* beyond its story: *Fiddler on the Roof* is about the breakdown and evolution of tradition in modern society; *Into the Woods* is about community and responsibility; *How to Succeed in Business Without Really Trying* is about the madness of corporate America; *The Fantasticks!* is about how the joys of growing up are not achieved unless pain is involved too ("Without a hurt, the heart is hollow"); as the King would say, "Et cetera, et cetera, et cetera." And everything in the show—every event, every character—needs to inform the theme . . . and vice versa.

However: one of the most common, yet oh-so-subtle problems that can beset a gestating musical is the point at which it shifts from what you *thought* it was about to what it's *really* about. When he was alive and running the BMI Workshop, Lehman Engel used to insist that the opening number be among the very *last* things you write for your show, as only then can you know exactly what show you're trying to set up. The point where you feel painted into a corner, or as if nothing you write is quite good enough to put you over the top, is a terrific time to reexamine your musical and see if it hasn't grown into something else when you weren't looking.

Selling Point #7: The planting of seeds and the avoidance of waste. Just as it's vital to set up permissions, it's equally vital *not* to set up false expectations. In other words, don't introduce a character, a very specific biographical/backstory detail, a significant character trait *unless you intend to pay it off at some point in the evening, in some way that propels the story forward and/or impacts upon its resolution.* Consciously and unconsciously, audiences keep track of these elements, and if any of them are unrelated or left dangling, you're not structuring (or even telling) your story properly.

Perhaps the most iconic example of this is the introduction of the Beggar Woman in *Sweeney Todd*, whose deceptive "recurring gag" cameo appearances carefully and cannily prepare for the eventual revelation of her true identity at the denouement (and no, I won't spoil it here; if you don't know it, shame on you, and get either of the DVD versions as fast as you possibly can). Credit original playwright Christopher Bond and adapting librettist Hugh Wheeler for the construction—and Sondheim for abetting it with an infamous musical clue.

A more subtle—and *terribly* interesting—example is librettist Peter Stone's portrayal of Judge James Wilson in *1776*. His appearances are sort of a running gag, too. A member of the Pennsylvania delegation, he is presented as a man who wants to avoid controversy as much as possible; which, positioned as he is between American-independence proponent Benjamin Franklin and stick-by-England conservative John Dickinson, often puts him in awkward circumstances. Throughout most of the show, though, Wilson remains intimidated enough to defer to Dickinson.

But this character trait suddenly pays off big time when the final vote for independence comes. After vigorous debate, leading to much amendment of the Declaration of Independence, so boldly drafted by Thomas Jefferson, all the colonies have voted yea but two: New York (an abstention)—and Pennsylvania.

The head Pennsylvania delegate, John Dickinson, expresses mild regret for "all of the inconvenience that such distinguished men as Adams, Franklin and Jefferson were put to just now. They might have kept their document intact, for all the difference it will make. Mr. President, Pennsylvania says—"

And Franklin cuts him off. Having just seen Delaware cast its yea by a pointedly articulated two-to-one majority among its delegates (another seed, carefully planted), he's struck by a sudden inspiration—and requests that the Pennsylvania delegation be polled, to likewise ascertain *its* majority sympathies.

Dickinson objects, but to no avail. It's a proper request.

Franklin votes yea.

Dickinson votes nay.

Poor Judge Wilson is suddenly *trapped* in the spotlight.

And all eyes turn to him.

Franklin: "There it is, Mr. Wilson, it's up to you now—the whole question of American independence rests squarely on your shoulders. An entirely new nation, Mr. Wilson, waiting to be born or to die in birth, all on your say-so. Which will it be, Mr. Wilson? Every map-maker in the world is waiting for your decision!"

Dickinson tries to put the pressure on. But this time Wilson yields to an even bigger pressure. Referring to Adams and Franklin, he says: "If I go with them, I'll be only one among dozens; no one will ever remember the name of James Wilson. But if I vote with you, I'll be the man who prevented American independence. I'm sorry, John—I just didn't bargain for that."

Wilson casts his vote: yea.

And the Declaration of Independence is adopted.

Why is this beat so interesting, aside from the fact that it just makes for terrific drama?

Because librettist Peter Stone (with composer-lyricist-historian Sherman Edwards, who wrote the score and conceived the show) made it up.

For all the overwhelming proportion of the show's events and characters that are historically accurate and documented, the historical explanation for *this* crucial turnabout is chronicled *nowhere*. There is no record as to why Judge Wilson suddenly changed his allegiance. Only that he did. At its academic best, the beat in the play is a hypothetical extrapolation.[4]

But read the whole show or watch the lovely new DVD of the reconstructed film adaptation (avoid the shorter, two-hour VHS cassette-tape release which reflects the movie-theatre version bowdlerized by producer Jack Warner). Clock how Stone set it up. Look what Stone did with it. And take note of how he made every deceptively small step along the way *count*.

Selling Point #8: Exoticism of the universe—or locale or backdrop, however you like to think of it, however it most applies to your show.

Most successful and/or interesting musicals are set in times and places far away from everyday contemporary life (look at the list in the section on main characters, p. 28). The ability of the musical to take us to otherworlds—of its music and poetic language to *evoke* those worlds—is key to the magic that sets it apart from any other art form. Indeed, as an elevated form, the musical naturally gravitates to elevated environments, just as it encourages larger-than-life main characters.

---

4. There is more to be found about how ingeniously Stone and Edwards adapted the facts of history while remaining assiduously true to the spirit, in an authors' afterword to the published libretto.

It's rarely a good idea to set a musical in a contemporary, present-day setting. Well, let me amend that: it's rarely a good idea *if part of your artistic objective is longevity.* Aside from the usual incongruity between the language of the prosaic and the poetic, you don't have the benefit of social and historical perspective that allows you to set your musical universe in thematic relief—and to look at its era free of contemporary mores that almost never date well. (Locales like offices and house/apartment rooms compound the problem, because they imply spaces that are closed and constricted. A choreographer once told me, "With its TV, family couch, end tables, all that crap, my worst nightmare is trying to create a peppy high-step around the den!")

Urban settings are especially vulnerable: The libretti for both *Company* (a stylistic trailblazer) and *Promises, Promises* (a foursquarely traditional tuner) are *painfully* dated; most of *Company*'s once-hip perceptions about married life have been rendered either quaint or, in the wake of increasingly sophisticated sitcoms, familiar . . . and in the case of *Promises,* while Neil Simon's book retains most of its "funny," the attitude toward women is, by today's standards, *appalling.* Even the cheerfully giddy satire *How to Succeed* can't quite conquer a milder and more knowing presentation of women as sex objects; and no less than the venerable Shakespeare-derived *West Side Story*—a worthy classic in so many ways, and a model of compact construction—can seem, because of its invented "youth slang" (ironically, devised to *free* it of ties to era locution), self-conscious and inauthentically "precious" in revival.[5]

I hasten to add: if you are *driven* to musicalize a certain contemporary story or theme, you *must* follow your muse (as dated as *Company* is, look at all the innovation that has occurred in its wake; no one says it was *unnecessary*). But if part of your plan is the long afterlife that comes with stock, amateur, and revival productions, don't proceed without much soul-searching. And when you do proceed, go at it with gusto, and look for ways to transcend the setting.

---

5. The mostly faithful film adaptations of dated shows often seem timeless because they bring with them the spirit, sensibility, and playing style of their era—to say nothing of the energies and personæ of the actors and creators for whom those attitudes figured into daily life. This ability to endow what would become dated material with *time-capsule legitimacy* is part of *film's* magic, because film preserves a moment frozen in history. Performing live is a whole different game, because there's no way to keep current sensibilities totally away from the delivery . . . or excise them from the audience that brings them into the theatre.

Selling Point #9: Believability of the universe. As a corollary, verisimilitude should never diminish, even if you leave the "real world" behind for a more fanciful one.

Take a look at the late Douglas Adams' brilliant science fiction parody *The Hitchhiker's Guide to the Galaxy* in its radio, LP, book, or TV incarnations (avoid the film). As outrageous as the characters, situations, and premises are, once Adams sets up the ground rules governing his wacky universe, he adheres to them assiduously (or assiduously enough that you never catch him in a story-logic violation).

Want a musical? Sondheim and Lapine's *Into the Woods*, set in a universe of interacting Grimm's fairy tales, is very nearly as impeccable. The use of magic has rules, limits, consequences, and the story honors them.

Conversely, there's *Finian's Rainbow*. It's largely unproduceable now (concert stagings aside); the book by Fred Saidy and the show's lyricist E. Y. Harburg has thus far been resistant to contemporary attempts at revision—but I don't think the structural clumsiness and dated thematic approach to the material is wholly the reason. Going hand-in-hand, and deeper, is this flaw: The authors never honor the conventions of fantasy, and dramatize magic arbitrarily. Why can the Leprechaun Og change the racist senator (who's been turned black) into a paragon of humanism without using one of his three wishes, but not turn him white again? The limits of Og's power are mutable, blurrily defined, and at the mercy of what the authors are trying to say at any given time. And the lack of consistency creates a lack of authenticity.

A phenomenon of the era in which we live has brought about another consideration, too. *Because* media and technology have made audiences so savvy about storytelling conventions, *the further you get from verisimilitude, the closer you get to camp.* And while camp can be fun—even lucrative, if you have the rare mind-set that can tap into an audience-grabbing special-material gimmick like *Forever Plaid* and *Nunsense*—it flies in the face of good musical structure because its very *raison d'être* is often stylistic anarchy.

The one notable exception to this observation is *Little Shop of Horrors*, which retains its structural integrity throughout, while parodying the horror genre to outrageous extremes. Ironically, it accomplishes this balance by being very faithful to the original Roger Corman B-movie and its already satirical screenplay by Charles Griffith. The campiness of the musical is not interpolated or imposed with arch superiority—it is, rather, organic to the very property itself and presented without editorial bias or self-consciousness. Librettist-lyricist Howard Ashman and composer Alan Menken merely—and deftly—place Mushnick's flower shop within the musical ambience of Phil Spector 1960s pop rock that is itself *an automatic reflection* of the original film's era.

Selling Point #10: The ending restores balance. In many cases, this has come to mean a happy ending—but not always. A musical can be a tragedy, but its ending needs to point toward hope. This is not an arbitrary aesthetic imposition, nor a mindless holdover from pure "musical comedy" but, again, a by-product of the form being so elevated and felt (at its best) so viscerally. It's fine to take the audience on a darker journey, *but you have to reward them for the effort of going on the ride.* When Sweeney Todd is killed by Tobias, the force of anarchy in the universe is stilled. Even though Tony is killed by Chino's bullet in *West Side Story,* the tragedy brings the warring factions together. Don Quixote dies as he begins to rally from ignominious defeat; but his dream will clearly live on in Sancho—and in the former whore Aldonza who proclaims, "My name is Dulcinea."

THE EXCEPTIONS THAT AREN'T

Nearly all "inviolate" principles of the sort described above have what we've all come to know as "exceptions that prove the rule"—because, when examined carefully, the elements that *seem* contradictory are actually camouflaging the elements that support the by-laws.

The arguably iconic exception is famously created by William Finn's one-acts *March of the Falsettos* and *Falsettoland,* which, when performed together, appear under the title *Falsettos.*

March of the Falsettos opened in 1980, *Falsettoland* ten years later; each is *wholly* a reflection of its time *and* each is largely set in various New York City apartments. How is *Falsettos,* alone among these others, immune to the guiding principles?

It's not.

Both plays are about the ways in which the traditional nuclear family has been redefined by divorce, sexuality, and other factors. The first play is about that specifically, the second adds the factor of AIDS (which is never referred to by name) to the equation. Timely issues, yes—but also timeless, because the issue of family redefinition in an increasingly informed society is not one that will ever go away; in fact it can only continue to evolve. Far from being dated, the issue has a built-in immortality. (Whereas 1970's *Company* might be—and has been—described as a "contemporary look at relationships," specifically marriage. And the relevant particulars of that *do* change as trends and social politics change.)

As for *Falsettos'* seemingly prosaic locales, such as Marvin's apartment, Mendel's office, Whizzer's hospital room: owing to the template imposed by James Lapine's original production, very few of these locales are designed in representational detail: chairs, tables, counters, whip on and off quickly, suggesting rather than spelling out; we can suddenly find ourselves in a nonlinear limbo (where a number of the songs take place, such as the first play's title number as well as its opening, "Four Jews in a Room, Bitching"), and the aesthetic feeling is never that of enclosure, but of open free-association.

And that's because the locales aren't presented literally, or omnisciently; rather, they emerge *primarily* from the main character Marvin's perspective (even when he isn't onstage, his view of the world seems to prevail). In other words: the milieu is the landscape of our hero's mind, his changing psychology. The rooms are but convenient symbolic reference points. Thus, seemingly prosaic elements are transformed into exotica.

That said, do I think Finn, who seems to write in a nonanalytic white heat, or Lapine, who's *very* into analysis, considered any of that *consciously?* Certainly Finn less than Lapine, but I doubt either one gave specific thought to How They'd Accommodate Traditional Principles in an Untraditional Piece. They were exploring new territory and the experiment, I'm sure, was enough to occupy them.

But such transcendence, by providence, coincidence, *gestalt,* or design, needs to occur. Because that's how musicals "speak" to audiences, and that's what keeps musicals alive in the literature.

And—to anticipate the question—no, it doesn't matter that Finn and Lapine (or anyone else) may honor the selling points "accidentally," nor that a cogent analysis of why their piece works is made only retrospectively. As history has proven time and again, artists don't necessarily know precisely what they're doing (or *everything* they're doing) when they do it—if they did, *instinct, whimsy,* and just plain *trying things on for size* would never play a part in the process. Just as you can't second-guess the marketplace, you shouldn't censor yourself from taking a risk.

But the examples set by well-regarded exceptions should *never* be taken as a rationale to ignore the basics. They are, however, precedent for experimenting with untraditional pathways (pathways recommended more for the seasoned musical theatre mind than the one still learning the essential vocabulary). But make such experimentation a *very* carefully considered *choice*, not a blind gamble.

IT'S NOT ALL TALK

All right. You have your list of recommended, classically proven "ingredients." But you don't just add dialogue and stir.

Most of you know that the dialogue is not the book, that it is merely a *feature* of the book. The book is the plot, the structure, the road map of thematic intent.

In the normal gestation of a libretto, it *will* start out as an unmusicalized script. But as songs are added, as it goes through the process of development (e.g., staged reading, workshop, tryouts), the book becomes increasingly refined and less obviously "visible." How much it "disappears" depends upon the style of the show and the proportion of music to dialogue.

But do understand something:

Songs "eat" book.

And they should.

Whether or not the librettist is also his own lyricist (and therefore, of course, coauthor of the score), the songs are not dropped into the book, but rather *absorb* the book—or *take over* from the book—at places of key emotion, intensity, or thematic importance. This absorption bespeaks an integration so thorough that the absence of song from a finished script will render it unintelligible. (And by the way, librettists, unless you are also functioning as the official lyricist, *never* indicate in your initially unmusicalized scenes Where the Songs Go, or What You Think the Songs Are—and for God's sake *never* include a dummy or model lyric. Finding and devising the songs is for the songwriters to do, and if your collaborators are sufficiently talented, they'll be more interesting, resourceful, and inventive about it than you will, because they're more schooled and practiced in recognizing elements that sing and motivate song; and in how to bring the craft of music and lyrics to bear. If you feel *strongly* about a certain speech or passage being musicalized, overwrite it a little. Your songwriters will *always* get the hint and respond to it—one way or another—appropriately.)

High points of story, emotion, and character development, in *most* cases, define the placement of songs within a score. A given song or musical sequence can develop a newly introduced idea or move the story forward—but the one thing it must never do is *repeat information we already know.* (And don't talk to me about "Betrayed" from *The Producers.* As hugely entertaining as Mr. Brooks' show is [and I am an unabashed fan], it's a comic parlor trick peppered through with novelty numbers.)

Simple deduction tells us that stock-in-trade for any libretto is *economy.* Where anything from 50 to 90 percent (or more!) of the evening may become sung material, the ability to communicate both simple and complex situations and characters in brief, bold strokes is essential.

This is achieved in a number of ways.

- The characters must be idiosyncratic, per the above, to make impact quickly.

- Also per the above, every scene and song in the show should somehow serve to further develop the underlying theme. (Stephen Sondheim and Harold Prince have occasionally, when interviewed, confessed that part of their process is for each of them to hold a *private* idea about what a given show metaphorically represents. Neither tells the other what it is, but each tries to follow it through all the way. Thus, for Sondheim, *Sweeney Todd* was about obsession; while for Prince it was about impotence. And if you examine every main character in the piece, *each is in relentlessly fervent pursuit of something she or he cannot have.* And most of the songs are about that too.)

- Exposition needs to be a function of—and as much as possible, camouflaged by—conflict. Via argument, debate, the collision of hero and obstacle. *This allows backstory and setup to be established through forward dramatic motion and relationships in action.* An oft-cited principle is *Exposition as ammunition.* Larry Gelbart's variant dictum is *No exposition except in anger.* Look at the libretti for most classic or important musicals and take note of how *quickly* and *efficiently* essential exposition is dealt with, using this principle. (Arthur Laurents' first dress shop scene early in the first act of *West Side Story* is the oft-cited model of exposition-through-conflict concision, setting up most of the show's intricately interconnected plot threads in a mere two pages.)

- For starting scenes, there's a screenwriting technique, first *popularly* codified as a principle, I believe, by William Goldman in his wonderful book *Adventures in the Screen Trade.* The top of any given scene should begin *as late into its action as possible.* In other words—enter at the point furthest into the scene at which everything that came *before* can be implicitly understood. Trust the audience's ability to *infer* a situation from dynamics already in progress. For example:

When John Adams first confronts the Continental Congress in *1776*, they're already in session. He *interrupts* them, in order to *rant* at them *and call them to action,* and their response is "Sit Down, John," which tells us this is a familiar and frustrating dynamic on both sides, played out often before.

When Act One of *Sweeney Todd* ends, Mrs. Lovett and Sweeney have just finished singing "A Little Priest." We know that he will go on his revenge-fueled killing spree and that she will support him by disposing of the bodies as filling for her meat pies. When Act Two begins, Mrs. Lovett's pie shop is doing a thriving business and a likewise newly affluent Sweeney is having his *special* barber chair delivered to *his* shop above hers. The transition between the two points—the buildup of Lovett's business, Sweeney putting in the order for his chair—is something we never see. Rather, the customers singing "God, That's Good" while Lovett tends to them, and Sweeney supervising delivery (among other related actions) *implies* all that, and so clearly that the audience instantly fills in the blanks. (Just as significantly: the sudden change is one the audience finds vastly amusing. Most of us who are passionate about musicals know *Sweeney Todd* nearly or entirely by heart; but imagine, or remember, seeing it for the first time, and how delightful it was to encounter the change in the Lovett/Todd fortunes *suddenly.*)

While a musical script should not be able to withstand a number-ectomy, consider the things that *can* be sacrificed without loss to sense or theme or structure. There's a terrific story from a book I have about the making of the TV miniseries *Shōgun*, based on the late James Clavell's sprawling and brilliant novel set in feudal Japan, whose paperback edition clocks in at 1,210 pages. Producer-screenwriter Eric Bercovici read the novel four times cover to cover, trying to find the key to its dramatization. He finally proposed to Clavell that the story had to be told exclusively from the point of view of its main character, British explorer John

Blackthorne; what Blackthorne saw, we'd see; if Japanese was spoken that he didn't understand, we wouldn't be helped by subtitles. Any subplot not directly linked to Blackthorne's narrative thread would have to be considered extraneous. Clavell considered; and when he next met with Bercovici to discuss it, handed him a paperback copy of the novel, in which entire sections and paragraphs had been ripped or crossed out. All that remained was Blackthorne's arc. "All right," said Clavell. "It works." Bercovici kept the crudely "abridged" edition on his desk throughout the writing process.

POSTSCRIPT #1: THE SMALL, BOOK MUSICAL

In the pantheon of small, book musicals, the list of classics is astonishingly brief.

What I mean by *small* is off-Broadway standard: a cast of nine or under (even if the show did not, itself, originate off-Broadway). What I mean by *book musicals* is self-evident: scripted, structured stories, not revues.

What I mean by classic has very specific parameters. I don't mean just successful, as in *made its money back* or *turned a profit* or *had a healthy run.* I mean entered the standard stock/amateur repertoire to be produced continually ever since. Not a resume success, not an occasionally mounted novelty that earns its authors some walkin'-around money now and again. Rather the kind of success that supports you and yours—anywhere from securely to fabulously—for the rest of your life. Stupid money.

I hasten to add, I'm not *really* talking about money, except as a fortunate by-product.

I'm talking about impact.

And the elements it takes to *make* that impact.

Small with Gimmick

I want to dispense with a certain kind of small musical that must be acknowledged, yet cannot be encouraged, because it operates beyond the purview of accepted craft. This is what I call the "gimmick" or "special material" musical. It attains popularity by dint of having keyed into a funny idea that has some universal appeal; or the interests of a particular, adequately populous audience faction. "Special material" shows tend to feature just that, *special material,* in the television sense of "tailored to meet a specific need"—while tending to be very camp and pointedly satirical. And the audience needs to be at least casually familiar with the archetypes being parodied to be in on the humor. In a gimmick show, *style dictates content!* And principles of craft and construction often go out the window in favor of simply making the antics wilder as the evening progresses.

Successful "gimmick" book shows would also seem to be a phenomenon of off-Broadway: their brazen ideas organically lead to brazen execution, and a consciously-winking atmosphere of cheap-fun-on-the-cheap-side. The list of classics is small, and doesn't go much beyond *Nunsense, Forever Plaid, The Rocky Horror Show,* and *Ruthless.* If you have the mind-set or sensibility for this kind of writing and believe it to be your métier, then, as Culp and Cosby used to say in *I Spy,* "Go for yourself." A gimmick musical that hits is a money machine, but one that's totally at the mercy of your ability to "guess right," and elicits virtually no artistic respect. For another phenomenon of these shows is that neither they nor their creators are ever taken seriously as models for emulation or even discussion. And the particular lightning they engender tends not to strike twice.

You'll have earned the right to cry about it all the way to the bank, though. And nothing wrong if you find that to be enough.

Small with Pedigree

The list of small, classic book musicals that are *qualified* for discussion here is, likewise, an astonishingly small one. Strictly speaking, it should include *Little Shop of Horrors,* but that one, covered already, is an anomaly, because it requires a full set and the renting (or building) of the Audrey II puppets. (Arguably, *Avenue Q* may qualify in the same vein, but as it is still enjoying its Broadway and soon Vegas success, the stock/amateur jury hasn't even been put through voir dire yet.) Check out the rest of the list, though.

The Fantasticks!

I Do! I Do!

Falsettos

You're a Good Man, Charlie Brown

Godspell

Those were all I could come up with. (And strictly speaking, even *I Do! I Do!* is a reach, popularity-wise.) I asked a few colleagues. They couldn't think of others, either.

If you know them, think about them for a while. Spotting the commonalities?

The Fantasticks! (Jones, Schmidt) is a parable that tells you growing up happens, but not without pain, nor without inevitable maturity and new insight. It's performed on a practically bare stage. Supposed to be.

I Do! I Do! (Jones, Schmidt), based on Jan de Hartog's *The Fourposter,* is another cycles-of-life story, tracing the history of an "average" marriage, from honeymoon couple to elders finally selling the house to a new couple. The necessary set piece? The bed. Everything else is carry on, carry off. The visuals are icons. Two characters.

Falsettos (Finn, Lapine), also covered earlier in this chapter. Scenery is similarly minimalist and modular. Deals with the universal subject of *what defines family.*

You're a Good Man, Charlie Brown (Gesner)[6], in which each act presents a day in the life of the title character and the rest of the *Peanuts* comic strip gang, created by Charles M. Schulz. A sort of world in microcosm, the Peanuts omniverse explores the universal verities of the human condition with its own distinctive spin. Platforms, boxes, Snoopy's house (a box with a roof), those simple costumes made to look like the familiar garb (like good ol' CB's crooked-line shirt), some baseball bats, Lucy's football, Linus's blanket . . .

Godspell (Schwartz, Tebelack), based on *The Gospel According to St. Matthew,* the parables in sketches and song, performed by youthful clowns in contemporary, seemingly improvised, garb and makeup—with the actual Jesus story (which has a few songs of its own) as a linking device, mostly implied via impressionistic bits and routines, rather than narratively dramatized. Spiritual and yet nonreligious, irreverent reverence. A lovely balance. Its biggest set piece is a chain-link fence.

All very different from one another. And yet . . .

---

6. I must add here—when you examine this show as an example of writing and construction, go to the original mid-'60s version by Clark Gesner, which is sweet, smart, and subtle; not the horrifically doctored (and not by its author) Broadway distortion of the late nineties, which is a vulgarized atrocity. Yet I must point out . . . *both* now are regularly licensed out.

All of these shows deliberately and *specifically* utilize minimalist design physicality to evoke universal themes, the skill of the actors to fill up the stage by playing upon your imagination. They all zero in on a very small, specific group to suggest a very big, very complete world that resonates with universal symbolism. And each stage setting defines a theatrical never-never land, a magical limbo with no literal constraints, where things become other things and time and space and locale are fluid, malleable, limitless.

They can all be done inexpensively, by almost any theatre group with a piano. Most can be performed for audiences of all (or nearly all) ages.

The ones that aren't family fare per se are about family, which kind of balances things, appeal-wise. (As I write this, Jason Robert Brown's *The Last Five Years*, about the deterioration of a marriage—a sort of new-millennium answer to *I Do! I Do!* whose cast is also just one couple—has been heating up the stock/amateur circuit and shows potential for making the list, too.)

Now . . . is it possible to aim for a show that uses this minimalist vocabulary and miss hitting? Of course. But there tend to be reasons why.

The biggest, of course, is that the show simply isn't good enough. Jones and Schmidt failed with *Celebration*, which is coy and cutesy and ultimately silly, despite a catchy score. They failed again with *Philemon*, which is only the *best* thing they've ever written, but was thwarted by numerous industry/timing forces weirdly conspiring to defeat public awareness. A very idiosyncratic case, though.

Others like *Violet, Floyd Collins, The Last Sweet Days of Isaac, Your Own Thing, I'm Getting My Act Together and Taking It on the Road*, et al. met with varying degrees of initial approval, up to and including significant off-Broadway runs. But for any number of reasons—subject matter not universal enough, scores not accessible enough, too difficult to produce in a semiprofessional or amateur venue (either because of limited resources or performance ability)—these shows don't move into the rarefied company of that very short list I've mentioned. And that's not to criticize them.

It takes time for patterns to emerge from history. And even if it didn't, who would tell the creators of those "off the list" shows not to work on them?

Not I.

I have one in the planning stages now that strikes me as a very long shot to make that list, itself.

You go where the passion is.

But if your passion can embrace the now-identified incorporation of symbolic, universal resonance as part of your *conscious* plan . . . not as something to pander to (for then you will fail), but as something to *aspire* to . . . isn't it worth considering?

POSTSCRIPT #2: NEW-AGE EXCEPTIONS

There is one other kind of musical structure to know about that demands separate consideration. I won't say that I don't recommend it, but it's fraught with peril, and the examples of success are very few. It has no "official" name; the ones I give here are my own, and so are all the related terms that follow; but they provide easy and, I think, accurate reference.

This is the *Group* musical, one that follows a group of characters with no single individual as focus.

The *Group* musical breaks down into two subcategories.

The first is the *Gestalt* musical. In this one, rather than having a single character pursue a goal, you follow a group of characters *who all individually want the* same *goal,* and the show dramatizes the variations of approach and motivation. It is the singularity of goal that creates dramatic unity, and the gestalt mentality substitutes for the drive of a main character. It is most effectively demonstrated by *A Chorus Line* (in which each dancer is after the job, as per "God I Hope I Get It"); and in *Assassins* (in which each of the gun-toters wants validation and recognition for his or her outrage and sense of disenfranchisement from the American dream).

The second is the *Panorama* musical. This type of musical follows *multiple storylines tied together by a single event or a single locale,* not dissimilar in its way to an epic potboiler novel. As far as I'm aware, there are only seven in the canon worth discussing—two *event,* three *locale,* and two that qualify as *crossovers.* Not all have been commercially successful (i.e., have made their money back as of this writing), but all are so widely acknowledged as standard literature that artistic success is a worthy enough qualification.

The two *event* ones are

1. *Pacific Overtures* (Sondheim, Weidman)—the panorama musical I like best, because it's so bracingly exotic and so richly written, with a matchless score. In it, we observe what happens to feudal Japan *after* the incursion of the Western world.

2. *Ragtime* (McNally, Flaherty, Ahrens) based on the moderate-length but epic-scope novel by E. L. Doctorow, which is about how significant points in early twentieth-century American history ripple out to affect the desires and actions of regular citizens (white, black, and immigrant) and dramatizes how several seemingly disparate storylines are related because they *converge* upon a single *coming* event.

The three *locale* ones are

3. *Follies* (Sondheim, Goldman) in which former stars of the Weissman (read: Ziegfeld) Follies and their significant others reunite at the theatre, which is about to be torn down, for a farewell party—during which they will relive old memories and resolve old (yet still current) issues.
4. *Titanic* (Stone, Yeston) which is of course about the passengers on the doomed ship.
5. *Grand Hotel* (Wright, Forrest with additional material by again, Stone and Yeston) based on the potboiler by Vicki Baum about a hotel in Berlin, circa 1928.

The crossovers are

6. *Into the Woods* (Sondheim, Lapine), in which various characters from Grimm's fairy tales (and two Grimm-*like* characters of the authors' own invention, the Baker and his wife) venture into an enchanted forest on various conflicting quests but ultimately must bond against a common enemy.
7. *Baby* (Maltby, Shire, Pearson), about three adult couples in a university town—very young, thirtyish, and middle-aged, respectively—each of which is expecting a baby; and about the impact this has on their lives, with regard to their individual *times* of life.

I suppose, if pressed, I'd have to admit that the wildly successful *Rent*—Jonathan Larson's update of *La Bohème*—might fit in here too, but that one is a notorious exception to *any* rule, a contemporary rock novelty left in structural disarray due to the untimely death of its author the night before its first off-Broadway preview. Though I admire aspects of it, I'm not a big fan of the show—but I have no argument with its proponents or its triumphs. I can only assert that, for purposes of studying the craft, it's a *total* anomaly, and can't be used as a general paradigm. And *Show Boat* has undergone such constant posthumous revision and restructuring with each mainstream revival that there's no accurate generalization to be made.

Why is the *Group* musical to be undertaken only with great caution?

First: It's expensive. Unless you conceive your epic story to be told by a small cast in multiple roles, employing Story Theatre-type techniques, you're looking at a show that *by definition* has no place in off-Broadway-type environments and can *only* be produced in a large Broadway-type venue. (There have been times when large musicals have debuted off-Broadway; but in all such cases, this has been for a limited run, and a gamble by the producers that the reviews will be good enough to warrant a move to Broadway. Needless to say, this requires a great deal of producer faith, and the gamble is high risk indeed.)

Second: It's very difficult to keep a group musical compelling on an emotional level. You have to keep multiple–and perhaps at first *uncon-nected*–storylines in the air, give them all more or less equal weight, and still make the audience care about what they're seeing, curious as to how the stories will merge. *At the same time* you must also provide the audience with historical and/or cultural perspective, since the effect of the environment upon your characters will almost certainly be at the heart of the story. *At the same time,* you must provide a varied, cohesive score that is dramatically and musically gratifying. Even when songs move the story along—as most do, these days—time slows: song time moves more slowly than dialogue time. Musical numbers have to establish melody, setting, rhythm, a unifying thesis, and lyric patterns. And let's not forget choreography, an essential part of any group-musical tableau. Discounting intermission, figure your *actual playing time* is two hours and fifteen to twenty minutes, tops. (This isn't only an artistic matter, it's a business matter. In a professional New York venue, if a show that starts at 8:05 runs past 11:00, you're into union-mandated overtime.) Your time to establish clear, complex narrative is no more than half to two-thirds of that. Not a lot of minutes in which to make an audience care about multiple characters in multiple developing storylines . . . for that matter, not a lot of minutes to let the audience simply get their bearings. The wider and more populous the canvas, the fainter the rooting interest, and the less intimate the experience. The less intimate the experience, the harder to connect on an emotional level.

Third: You're at the mercy of the times. And I don't mean fads. I mean the unpredictable ways in which storytelling styles change with a changing culture; and maybe even current events. The group musical, no matter how well executed, only survives in a climate that's ready for what it specifically has to offer.

Case in Point #1: *Pacific Overtures,* an acknowledged masterpiece, only ran six months on Broadway in 1976 (193 performances, to be exact). The imperialistic attitude of the West was not nearly so hot a topic as it is now, and perhaps more critical that that, *many audience members found the multiple stories and characters confusing.* Not for any want of clarity on the part of the authors or the production—audiences simply weren't used to the technique. But something startling happened in American entertainment between *Pacific Overtures* and every other *Panorama* musical previously listed:

Television writer-producer Steven Bochco and his groundbreaking cop drama, *Hill Street Blues,* which he cocreated with Michael Kozoll.

The pilot was broadcast on Thursday, January 15, 1981 at 10:00 p.m. When the hour was over, television had changed forever.

Producer-writer Bochco's creation was a series about a beleaguered inner-city police station. It featured:

—over a dozen main characters—

—jagged camerawork—

—a verité style—

—continuing storylines that developed week after week—

—and at the hub, holding all the strands together, the central figure of Captain Francis Xavier Furillo, as marvelously personified by Daniel J. Travanti; the moral center to whom you could return, to give the universe its sense of cohesion.

We in the audience had grown well accustomed to the miniseries (such as the aforementioned *Shōgun*), but that format was a long, sprawling affair, unfolding at a measured pace, spread out over several consecutive nights. Even the so-called primetime soap (*Peyton Place, Dallas*) was comparatively leisurely. Bochco and his folks on the Hill, though, were giving us something else—an intense shorthand: 44 minutes a week in which to keep track of a whole squad room and the unnamed city in which it tried to keep the peace. We had to think fast to keep up. We had to be willing to shift gears several times *before* the act break. The show recalibrated the way we thought about drama: it crammed more information into less time, and *counted on you* to keep things straight, to go where it led, to stay clear and invested. And to return for more of the same the following week.

Hill Street Blues ended its run in 1987, its effect on the media having had by then more than half a decade to operate. That same year *Into the Woods* opened. Two years later, *Grand Hotel* became an unexpected hit. Whether or not these musicals were consciously influenced by the Bochco-created ripple is not just debatable, but doubtful, considering their creative histories. But I don't think the *subconscious* influence—the era in which they were developed—can be ignored. And I don't think it's a coincidence that, in spite of mixed reviews, audiences were *primed* for the *Panorama* musical in a way they hadn't been before. The game had changed.

But now television and entertainment in general are surfeited on the style that *Hill Street Blues* pioneered. It's become so much the norm that the challenge has become keeping it fresh.

The game could change again. For, coming full circle, the Roundabout Theatre mounted a Broadway revival of *Pacific Overtures* in late 2004, a breathtaking production directed by Amon Miyamoto, reproducing the staging and concepts of a production he originated in his native Japan. Highly anticipated, well-reviewed. . . .

And over after sixty-nine performances.

Case in Point #2: When *Assassins* originally opened off-Broadway, in 1990, the vocabulary of the *Gestalt* musical had been well established by the monster hit *A Chorus Line*. Yet the reviews for *Assassins* were mostly negative. Because of the pedigree of the creative team (Sondheim in particular, and Jerry Zaks was the director), you couldn't get *near* the limited run (seventy-three performances) at Playwrights Horizons, but due to bewildered reviews and a political climate colored by the Gulf War, interest in moving it to Broadway evaporated like morning dew. But in spring 2004, the Roundabout Theatre opened a revival at Studio 54 on Broadway (a much larger house) to rave reviews—from many of the same critics!—and even a few Tony awards.

In examining the erosion of the American dream and the anarchic mentality bent on destroying perceived oppressors by dint of violence,

Assassins, fueled by 9/11, the Bush *fils* administration, and the RCA Victor original cast CD (which gave us all—pro, con, and newbie—ample time to get the score into our hearts, heads, and bones) meant a whole helluva lot more to audiences than it had fourteen years before.

And in the end, the lauded and lovely *Assassins* revival *still* closed after 101 performances.

As I said earlier, none of this means you should avoid the group musical. If you feel compelled, it may be with good reason.

But this book is about *surviving* as a musical theatre writer, and surviving means understanding the odds and acknowledging the logistics involved in bucking them. At least until you're an established player who can afford to take the long shot, perhaps even with some financial and producer support, the projects you generate on your own have the best chance of making it through the various stages of development and production if they're of manageable size and traditional structure.

You can almost always save epic ambitions for later.

POSTSCRIPT #3: THE EURO-MUSICAL

The long-running popularity of *Les Misérables, Miss Saigon,* and *The Phantom of the Opera,* among others, has been an unfortunate influence on some young musical theatre writers, because it encourages didacticism, bombast, lack of subtext, operatic pretension, and music bereft of pastel shadings. The lyrics are often abysmal, and the books sketchy (*Phantom*) or confusing (*Les Miz*), and in general stage spectacle is at the forefront, rather than theme, story or character. In a very real sense the juggernaut shows popularly labeled *Euro-musicals* are push-button entertainment machines—they chug through their paces from performance to performance with conveyor-belt regularity and scant regard to audience reaction (as opposed to audience attention, which they hold), the theatrical equivalent of theme parks.

All of which sounds like a put-down. Believe me or not . . . it isn't. I wouldn't dare.

You cannot argue with the unprecedented success these shows have had, nor put on superior airs about them. I know a lyricist who refused to see *Cats* even once during its entire eighteen-year run in New York. And I think he's the lesser artist for willful ignorance. *You must always learn the landscape.*

Nor am I saying these shows aren't enjoyable to those of us hard-wired to sing differently (I've liked a few myself, sometimes in *spite* of myself)—and I don't mean to imply that seeing them should feel like the homework assignment that it may well be for you. You're like as not to have a ball.

But Euro-musicals must nonetheless be acknowledged as a separate animal—borne of a distinctly non-American, even opera-house sensibility, utilizing a different vocabulary, employing few fresh or untried writing voices, and all generated by producing entities with enough money and power to support the excess (Andrew Lloyd Webber's Really Useful Company, Cameron Macintosh, and others).

And current survival rates suggest that Euro-musicals may be an era-specific phenomenon. In New York, the long runners from the eighties are gone (*Cats, Les Miz, Miss Saigon*), save one that earns its steadily-treading keep as tourist fare (*Phantom*[7]), and the new generation entries are proving to have little or no staying power, some even closing out of town. And the high profile of imitation-Euro writer Frank Wildhorn, an all-Amurricun boy, is misleading. To date, none of his shows, not even *Jekyll and Hyde,* has recouped its investment.

Why are new Euros meeting with less and less popularity? I think it's because when Euro-musicals were first making their presence known, their particular brand of spectacle-accented simplicity was borne of honest theatrical experimentation. Like them or not, they featured the authenticity of a newly discovered musical theatre locution.

But the sameness of their insistent, loud, broad strokes soon established itself as a trademark gimmick of the genre, rife for unintentional self-parody. Once the innocence of genuine discovery was gone, Euro-musical traits represented either cynical, mercenary calculation; or a bag of tricks that had worn out its range and welcome. At which point audiences became hip to the pandering. As they always eventually will.

I hasten to add, I have no wish to cubbyhole all *European-bred* musicals out of hand—for there are some interesting ones out there that America has never encountered—merely to categorize what we've come to know

---

7. The popular, award-winning American touring *Phantom*s, both the mainstream version by Arthur Kopit and Maury Yeston, and the Young Audience version by Rob Barron and myself, are not to be confused with Lloyd Webber's in content or style. Each telling of the tale is radically distinct from the others and—most important for this discussion—the USA versions are rooted in traditional American musical theatre conventions all the way.

and expect as Euro-musical *trademarks,* with the term "Euro-musical" used to define the idiosyncratic school of writing that promulgates them.

That said, however, the best Euros have indeed been carefully refined to hold audience attention and maintain focus—but only in accordance with their foursquare parameters. The notoriously erudite lyricist Richard Maltby, Jr., who (unsurprisingly) wrote the most artful English lyrics for any Euro, providing one of the genre's clearest and most character-coherent libretii, *Miss Saigon* (collaborating with the French team of Boublil and Schönberg, to whom Maltby affectionately refers as "The *Les Mizzes*") told a BMI class, speaking dryly, "I tried to inject my signature sophistication, cleverness, and wordplay into *Miss Saigon*—and boy did [the show] *not want it.*" Stylistically, and in terms of learning the craft, Euros symbolize a severely limited palate, and do not present a paradigm for emulation.

Enjoy them (if you can), admire them (if you do), take from them whatever inspiration seems useful or motivating (the energy and showmanship can be exhilarating) . . . but do *not* follow in their footsteps.

The widely known Euro-musical template is a deceptive anomaly.

Like any other siren song, hers will only lead you astray. . . .

5

CHAPTER

Knowing the Score
or:
Music and Lyrics

THERE ARE INDIVIDUAL PRINCIPLES GUIDING THE DISCIPLINES
of music and lyrics, but in musical theatre they must always be considered together. Even if you write only one, you must understand the basics
of the other, because their interdependence is the key.

Since this is a *survival guide* rather than a *primer*, I'm not going to put
forth a curriculum or a program of study; I'm going to assume you're
pursuing that on your own. I'll do a little cursory overviewing by way of
putting basic terms (AABA, Verse-Chorus, etc.) into the *philosophical* context of why certain song forms are survival aids . . . but if you're truly not
conversant with those forms, or are just learning craft principles from
scratch, do augment what's here with at least one other reputable book,
course, or class or that's dedicated to covering song structure in depth.[1]

---

1. The best such class remains the three-plus-year songwriters program of the BMI-
Lehman Engel Musical Theatre Workshop (www.bmi.com/musicaltheatre/
lengel.asp), the First Year especially, where the basics are concerned. Because of my
own long-term association with the Workshop, I have taken pains here not to reproduce lessons, examples, or approaches that have been codified and developed by
other members of the faculty (though of course the immutable principles of craft are,
however differently presented, consistent), so if you audition and get accepted, you
will find it a wholly worthwhile (perhaps even life-altering) experience unique unto
itself. The program is offered free, and to my knowledge constitutes the only one
around that provides reliable, firm grounding for the aspiring musical dramatist,
plus dedication to developing and nurturing individual writers over the long haul.
Contrary to what its detractors (usually the proponents of other courses) have implied over the years, the BMI Workshop imposes no philosophy save the commitment to excellence, and imposes no creative sensibility save persistence. (There is no

That emphasized, let's look at some songwriting basics, principles, and philosophies to help give your independent studies the most solid possible framework.

REFERENCE

First, equip yourself with at least one great thesaurus (Roget is, of course, the standard-bearer) and one great rhyming dictionary. The Clement Wood rhyming dictionary is often cited as the book of choice (and it contains essays on rhyme and poetic form that alone make it worth the price of purchase)—but the one I rely on principally is Jane Shaw Whitfield's (whose editor, Frances Stillman, is co-bylined), because—at least to me— its thoroughness, logic of organization, and ease of navigation trumps all others. (There are some reports that it has become hard to find, and indeed the once-ubiquitous first green, then yellow, Washington Square Press edition is out of print; but the Wiltshire Book Company of Hollywood, California, has rereleased it as *Songwriters' Rhyming Dictionary.* Wiltshire is a small, independent publisher, and there's no telling how long they'll be able to keep the book available; but I urge you to locate a used or new edition any way you can.)

FORM

The patterns imposed by standard forms are useful and time tested. Many a musical dramatist has experimented and succeeded with more complex and unusual structures after mastering the standard patterns (most famously Stephen Sondheim), but no musical dramatist has ever hurt his career by largely holding to them (Kander and Ebb, Jerry Herman, Bock and Harnick, and others).

Let's go over two standard song forms in dramaturgical terms by way of making the following case:

A song has to be graspable upon first listening.

(Footnote 1 continued)

such thing, for example, as "the typical BMI Workshop musical" which was once the pejorative of pundits who never attended the classes.) The BMI Workshop is simply the blue-ribbon standard-bearer for getting the message across and sustaining the art. It is also a place to meet other writers, network a little—and make a few lifelong friends. I'm not alone in being able to say that, literally, I'd have had no career worth discussing without it.

Poetry is a private affair between the reader and the page; it can afford to be dense, indirect, abstract; and it can be savored, mulled over, examined at leisure. Even today's pop songs, whose words can be as impressionistic as any poem, can be studied with a touch of the ASMS button on the CD player. But music and lyrics for the theatre are telling a story and exist in real time. And they have to do their *job* in real time. It's great if the material is rich enough to bring new rewards upon hearing it again—but if the gist, the point, the story are not clear first time through, you don't get a second chance.

Patterns of diction, of rhetoric (both musical and verbal)—patterns dictated by song forms—are what acclimate the ear. And despite their formality, they can, paradoxically, let you soar.

Okay, let's take AABA.

An A is a subject or title-line stanza. It codifies the argument, or thesis. And the first A in the chain introduces it.

The second A, exactly or nearly identical in melody and word pattern, expands upon it, develops it further.

The B is often called the bridge (a new section between As)—or sometimes, more evocatively, the *release*. Theatre songwriters sometimes talk of this section as the place where the song says *because* or *therefore* or *as opposed to.*

The third A, which may contain an extension or coda, brings the argument home.

The third A need not be final. You can add As and Bs as the story and/or emotional stakes demand (it is not uncommon to encounter AABABA, for example). But it gives a sense of wholeness to the song's musical and lyrical profile. Here's a very simple example excerpt by Stephen Sondheim, from *A Funny Thing Happened on the Way to the Forum,* with very short As and a short B, but no less eloquent for all that:

> (A) SOMETHING FAMILIAR,
> SOMETHING PECULIAR,
> SOMETHING FOR EVERYONE,
> A COMEDY TONIGHT.
>
> (A) SOMETHING APPEALING,
> SOMETHING APPALLING,
> SOMETHING FOR EVERYONE.
> A COMEDY TONIGHT.

    (B) NOTHING WITH KINGS!
          NOTHING WITH CROWNS!
          BRING ON THE LOVERS,
          LIARS AND CLOWNS!

    (A) OLD SITUATIONS,
          NEW COMPLICATIONS,
          NOTHING PORTENTOUS OR POLITE.
          TRAGEDY TOMORROW—
          COMEDY TONIGHT!

The alternate standard forms of Verse-Chorus and Verse-Verse Chorus define, in a way, the inverse dramatic approach. Since musical sections are alphabetically identified by which appear first, this form is often referred to as AB or AAB, respectively. But in *dramaturgical comparison* to AABA, the development of ideas is more like BA or BBA.

That's because the verse(s) is (are) a *warmup* to a title refrain. In other words, the verse material builds a case—the refrain is the conclusion drawn, or the codification of the thesis/argument. Here is an equally simple, but no less eloquent, example by Robert Lopez and Jeff Marx from *Avenue Q* (beginning songwriters note, this is a slightly advanced example, in which the verses and choruses expand their musical and lyrical motives upon repetition; in a more traditional example, the respective As and Bs would scan, and be set to melody, identically).

(A: Verse)   **BRIAN**
             WHEN I WAS LITTLE,
             I THOUGHT I WOULD BE . . .

             KATE MONSTER
    What?

              BRIAN
             A BIG COMEDIAN
             ON LATE NIGHT TV.
             BUT NOW I'M THIRTY-TWO
             AND AS YOU CAN SEE
             I'M NOT.

KATE MONSTER

Nope!

BRIAN

OH, WELL.

(B: Chorus)   IT SUCKS TO BE ME.

KATE MONSTER

Noooo.

BRIAN

IT SUCKS TO BE ME.

KATE MONSTER

No!

BRIAN

IT SUCKS TO BE BROKE
AND UNEMPLOYED
AND TURNING THIRTY-THREE.
IT SUCKS TO BE ME.

(Dialogue Interlude)   **KATE MONSTER**

Oh, you think your life sucks?

BRIAN

I think so.

KATE MONSTER

Your problems aren't so bad.

(A: Verse)   I'M KINDA PRETTY
AND PRETTY DAMN SMART.

BRIAN

You are.

KATE MONSTER

Thanks!

I LIKE ROMANTIC THINGS
LIKE MUSIC AND ART.
AND AS YOU KNOW,

I HAVE A GIGANTIC HEART,
SO WHY DON'T I HAVE
A BOYFRIEND?
FUCK! [2]

(B: Chorus)   IT SUCKS TO BE ME.

BRIAN

Me too.

KATE MONSTER

IT SUCKS TO BE ME.

BRIAN

IT SUCKS TO BE ME.
IT SUCKS TO BE BRIAN . . .

KATE MONSTER

AND KATE . . .

---

2. A quick caution: Profanity in lyrics is a very dicey device. Even though cusswords are now a pervasive part of everyday speech—for good or ill—setting them to music still has a way of emphasizing them all out of proportion to your intent. That's because music automatically elevates words set to it—thus, in most cases interpolating profanity has the effect of adding an intensifier to an intensifier. (Maury Yeston's phrase for a double-loaded device, derived, I suspect, from an early Dr. Seuss book, is "A hat on top of a hat".)

In *Avenue Q*, the profanity in "It Sucks to Be Me" is only mildly shocking, but earns its laugh because it sets up the authors' permission to be irreverent. Interestingly, too, according to Jeff Marx, "We didn't put it there to get a laugh. We put it there (extremely intentionally, by the way) early on in the first real song of the show, to set up the language of the evening, and demonstrate that Kate Monster isn't just a puppet, she's a modern, everyday PERSON like everyone else in the room, who sometimes curses in the course of everyday conversation. Actual examples of getting laughs based on the established permission to be irreverent would be the teacher's name, Mrs. Thistletwat, and the line in 'The Internet is for Porn,' 'GRAB YOUR DICK AND   DOUBLE-CLICK.'"

In *Assassins*, when Byck sings, "I DESERVE A FUCKING PRIZE," or in *Sweeney Todd*, when the barber sings, "THERE'S A HOLE IN THE WORLD LIKE A GREAT BLACK PIT/AND IT'S FILLED WITH PEOPLE WHO ARE FILLED WITH SHIT . . ." those are carefully selected expressions of rage. In my own "A Man" from *Weird Romance*, when the women conclude that men are incurably "fucked up," it informs a punch line by then well earned; and by the time we hear it, we're so comfortable with the conversational tone that it registers with its colloquial definition—confused and crazy—rather than as a scatological violation.

If you must use lyric profanity, do so judiciously. And when in doubt, find an alternative solution.

BRIAN
TO NOT HAVE A JOB . . .

KATE MONSTER
TO NOT HAVE A DATE!

BOTH
IT SUCKS TO BE ME!

(For more information about *Avenue Q*, see www.AvenueQ.com)

In AABA as well as Verse-Chorus, the more the arguments intensify, the more the music is enhanced as you go (through arrangement, compositional variation, or both), the hotter the song gets and the higher the energy. (Though there are occasions, usually comic ones, in which verbatim musical repetition is, ironically, the ante-upper, because it heralds new comic variations in the lyric, for example, "Everybody Ought to Have a Maid" or "Brush Up Your Shakespeare.") The repetition of shape is an insistent propulsion that keeps the audience focused and oriented even as new ideas are introduced.

As I said earlier, if you're adventurous enough and—importantly—if your show, by dint of subject matter and vocabulary, demands or suggests it . . . there's nothing wrong with a practiced musical dramatist, who (please) has mastery of the basics solidly under his belt, choosing to reach for, or even invent, bolder, less-predictable forms; forms that introduce Cs, Ds, Es and motivic variants, perhaps even ordered according to dramatic impulse rather than rigid alphabetic template.

But it's advisable to allow for *some* kind of graspable architecture. You venture into the realm of *arioso* (the kind of free-form composition that is often the staple of recitative in opera) at great risk. (For example, Adam Guettel and Tina Landau's *Floyd Collins* is a breathtaking and brilliant show; but woe betide the viewer/listener with a slow or conventionally attuned ear. The score is as difficult as it is ingenious; it offers no learning curve and takes no prisoners, and that has hurt its popularity and limited its stock and amateur productions.)

If you *must* venture out into "the deep end of the pool," try to structure your score overall so that it offers the listener some kind of orientation into its compositional ground rules. (As so often, Stephen Sondheim is the master of *this* too. For example, the opening bars of *Assassins* are a carnival carousel version of "Hail to the Chief"; the rest of the score, as it explores the history and psychology of successful and failed presidential assassins, likewise explores song genres that define the history of musical Americana. Even when the architecture is "explosive," the vocabulary of the familiar styles visited provides reference points; and the cohesive sound overall, whether you understand it academically or just somehow feel it, occurs because each song is based on some deconstructive variant of . . . you guessed it . . . "Hail to the Chief." By simply quoting the famous tune, Sondheim defines the musical ground rules right at the top.)

MELODY

One of the most useless tenets of musical theatre advice that you will be given ad nauseam is also one of the truest: You have to write strong melodies. There are not nearly enough good tunes in contemporary musicals, and one of the things that will help your work stand out notably is solid, muscular tunesmithery.

Easy to say. It's like a director telling an ingenue, "Act better."

But how the hell do you build on it, make sense of it in any practical, procedural way?

Well, let's accept a hard, ugly fact first.

Some people "get it" and some don't.

As with any art, the practitioner, when all is said and done, has to have the gift for it, the knack for it, *the connection to it.*

A mediocre "voice" can learn to improve . . . but never with the sharp, intuitive inspiration of the genuinely gifted one. And for those whose gifts rest between "good" and "genius," the potential for growth depends entirely upon a visceral connection with "The Show Biz," for infusing music with theatrical, situational muscle, and understanding that *muscle* need not simply mean *force* and *rhythmic energy,* but can also mean *passion* and *urgency*—even in the most delicate moments, by dint of sustaining musical and thus dramatic tension with selective spareness.

But let's say, for the sake of argument, that *that much* is in your belly.

Now let's talk tunes.

There are two kinds of tune makers.

The first and least are what I call "hummers," musical illiterates with a certain facile (and usually derivative) gift, who hum or sing their tunes to hired arrangers—arrangers who then, in turn, do the actual grunt work of composition, harmonization, and notation. There's nothing fundamentally wrong with being a hummer, and there are even a few hummer scores I'm fond of (*The Producers*, by Mel Brooks [the solely author-credited hummer] and Glen Kelly [the deceptively musical-supervision-credited worker bee], is one of them)—but it's a kind of musical chicanery all the same. Additionally, being a hummer limits the scope, reach, and versatility of one's creative ability. Having no meaningful mastery of, or acquaintance with, practical harmony, compositional development and styles, classical literature, and so on—and possessed of no academically understood or comprehensively studied mechanism with which to truly experiment—the hummer is restricted in vocabulary to the common song forms he knows, the conservative progressions that sound consonant to an untrained ear, and usually even dramatic broad strokes, since he has no working access to the full range of music's pastel shadings. Relatively speaking, the hummer's palate is a small one. If you're savvy enough to be an effective hummer (and don't kid yourself, *effective* hummers are a *tiny* minority), you're smart enough to acquire and make use of a musical education. Push yourself and aim higher. Not only does the world of musical theatre deserve it—so do you.[3]

The second kind of tune maker is the genuine, educated, trained, and comprehensive musician. Since he *does* have a full arsenal to draw upon, his challenge is to keep a certain accessibility alive, concomitant with delving into more advanced, adventurous territory. Even hugely gifted aspiring composers (especially young ones, fresh out of the gate and eager to make a mark) can charge with too much ferocity into music that has great compositional and dramatic integrity, yet doesn't register on the ears of enough listeners as memorable. So care must be taken not to confuse high musicianship with self-defeating rarefaction.

Now, *memorable* is a funny and charged word.

---

3. This is not to downplay the contribution that musical directors, orchestrators, vocal arrangers and dance music arrangers can make in *any* context, be it in the service of a "hummer" or a trained composer. Certainly they will manipulate and doctor a fully composed score far less, and only as far as the true composer requests and/or permits; but these specialists, especially if they have a real synergy with the composer, are absolutely invaluable problem solvers, who can do anything from taking over in areas where you don't have the expertise or time that lets you do it all yourself . . . to providing input critical to a number's most effective structure, texture, tempo, or musical vocabulary.

Sondheim has expressed his disdain of it, claiming that *memorable* is really just another word for *familiar*. Addressing a class in the very first year of the ASCAP Workshop in the early-eighties, he expounded upon this by pointing out that in older musicals of the twenties, thirties, forties, fifties, and even sixties, with lighter and less sophisticated dramatic needs, multiple reprises of songs were built into the machinery. You'd hear the forthcoming melodies in the overture. You'd hear them introduced fully in the show. You'd hear them developed in the dance music. You'd hear them in the entr'acte. You'd hear them reprised in Act Two. You'd hear them in the exit music. "And after all that," Sondheim said, "people would leave the theatre saying, '*God*, that man can write tunes!'" (Sondheim even makes a musical joke of this in *Merrily We Roll Along*. Virtually every tune the fictional composer Franklin Shepard writes is the same melody put through a different arrangement's filter. Upon hearing the tune for the first time—late in the backwards-moving musical, when Franklin and his lyricist collaborator Charley Kringas are just starting out—a producer advises them, in song, "You Need a Tune You Can Hum." Advice whose notes precisely echo those of the presumably unhummable ditty.)

Taking Mr. Sondheim's point, I respectfully disagree to *some* degree. As I discussed in the chapter on libretti, the rapid pace of media growth, and the commensurate innovations in media storytelling, have quickened our minds. We perceive a lot more a lot faster, which is *why* no one writes musicals "like they used to." You can't. We no longer even *think* that way. And there's no turning back. Even our fondest nostalgia is edged and knowing.

Thus *memorable* need not *always* mean "You can hum the tune walking out of the theatre" (though it's nice if you can have that too, and it's not a bad idea to shoot for it here and there). I think it's enough to mean that, somewhere in each major set piece, there is a motif that takes hold in a way whose repetition is anticipated, savored, and then lingers after the show is over—not because it's familiar, but because it's *distinct*. Possibly the song's title motif, but not necessarily. It may as effectively be a recurring one, that defines *a character's emotional state* or *an anthematic sentiment*, or *a transition to a new revelation*. In the abstract there's no clearer blueprint for how a memorable motif or melody is achieved—each specific song will evolve toward its specific makeup—but if you build your songs with such motivic development in mind, context will lead you. Remember always the axiom: Form follows function, and content dictates style.

Now . . . how do you make the motive or motives memorable?

It's in the confluence of these elements: distinctive rhythmic scan of key phrases, the way those phrases ride the melody, and a melody whose intervalic relationships uniquely support and emphasize the dramatic idea. And while the creation of this confluence cannot exactly be taught, it can be observed clearly enough to be emulated and refined with practice and care.

Take Jerry Herman's score for *La Cage aux Folles*. Listen to the way the male chorus revs up for the title line in the title song, that insistent four-note pattern. Naughty, isn't it? And the title—all on one note. By contrast, take the ballad "Look Over There," sung by a father to an errant son. Feel the urgency of the ¾ as Georges makes his case—feel the rising stakes as he gets to the title line, stated not once, but twice, the notes rising with the repetition.

Something subtler? Try the pointillistic development in "Finishing the Hat," from Sondheim and Lapine's *Sunday in the Park with George*. Note how the song sections keep expanding with the repetition of the notes that form the title phrase. Note how that device both musically echoes the pointillism of the main character George Seurat's painting style and also makes the philosophical case of a work of art that is built methodically, choice upon choice, detail upon detail.

Something less contained? "If I Were a Rich Man" by Jerry Bock and Sheldon Harnick from *Fiddler on the Roof*. Note how the wish is expressed in a little anthem; note too how the melody expresses not only the joy Tevye takes in the imagining, but also the sorrow of its hopelessness, plus the indigenous folk music of his culture, as it glides easily and expansively through major and minor modes.

Whenever you listen to a score—a theatre score, an opera score, a film score, an instrumental score—but *especially* a theatre score—*pay close attention to those signature moments.* Because those melodic silhouettes are what define a melody's "profile."

Think of their strength, their individuality, and above all, how each acts as a fingerprint-unique signature.

That is what you're aiming for.

The more you identify it, analyze it, concentrate on it, in the songs you love and learn (and learn to love), the more it will start to become a natural way of life for you. And the more willingly and ambitiously you will demand it of yourself. There are a few gifted writers of note who will quite outspokenly condemn this kind of "mercenary" approach as "pandering" or "selling out" or somehow being untrue to the loftier aims of certain adventurous musicals. To the best of my knowledge, though, none of these writers has ever had anything resembling a hit.

High-profile melodic content *transcends* the kind of show and characters you're trying to write, because in all cases, if you nail it, *it enhances them.* And then, to borrow a telling phrase, Everything's Coming Up Roses.

Why in your right mind would you pass *that* up?

MUSICAL PAINTING, OR: THE POETIC CONNECTION

Perhaps the most frustratingly unsatisfying theatre-intended songs to hear are those that employ the indicia of musical styles arbitrarily, or seem to employ no musical styles at all. Soft rock used solely to create energy, and what I call "church basement tonic-dominant" vamping used for generic liveliness, are the icons of this kind of composition, but there are others. Suffice it to say that the big sin for composers is writing *music without personality*—or music whose *imposed* personality is not organically derived from what's being dramatized.

The more you study musical theatre scores of all kinds, the more you'll find that with the best ones, the ones that stay in the literature and become classic, there is almost always a poetic connection between the music and the lyric and/or the drama of the lyric.

Now, what do I mean by a poetic connection?

It varies hugely: it can be a literal device that approximates a sound in nature or in technology—like the opening vamp of "Company" (Sondheim) that approximates a busy signal—or it can be philosophical, like the wide-open spaces evoked by the melodic sweep and spare accompaniment of "Oh, What a Beautiful Mornin'" (Rodgers, Hammerstein). It can be a comment by way of choosing the right genre—like "Brotherhood of Man" (Loesser) which puts a big gospel number in the world of big business; or it can be cultural, as in the way the indicia of Jewish folk music inform *Fiddler on the Roof* (Bock, Harnick). And there are countless other ways to achieve it.

But here's the point of it: The poetic connection is the reason that music is aesthetically wedded to its context; and it's often the difference between a perfectly nice score and a score that resonates. It's almost always the difference between a score that makes a mark and a score that's forgotten. There are dozens upon dozens of middling, midlist shows, even a few that were hits in their time, that are ignored now, because the scores are generic. I don't necessarily mean bland or ungifted or without the imprimatur of their authors . . . I mean lacking an overall character. *On a Clear Day You Can See Forever* (Lerner, Lane) is one; so's *New Girl in Town* (Merrill). We don't think about them much because they don't transport us. Even understanding the characters and the story, if you removed the lyrics from the music—the music wouldn't tell the tale.

Because music cannot always be discussed in a literal manner, musical painting is often a suggestive affair. You can't really explain why "Try to Remember" from *The Fantasticks!* (Jones, Schmidt) just *has* to be a gentle waltz—but you know that the gentle waltz evokes nostalgia for a simpler time. You can't really parse why "Do You Love Me?" in *Fiddler on the Roof* should be propelled by a single, pulsing quarter note for the question and simple chording for the answer—but you know it enhances the thoughts and feelings of delicate emotional intimacy. And why is soft-rock energy justifiable for *Pippin* (Schwartz)? Because there it enhances the notion of a populist never-never land, a place where old-world myth and history meet new-world whimsy.

Sometimes you *can* find *direct* word pictures. Look at the piano vocal score for "Pretty Women" in *Sweeney Todd*. Note the repeated A-natural quarter note that never seems to resolve; for all the beauty of the song, it never releases tension—and is that repeated quarter a metaphor for the pulse in the Judge's jugular as Sweeney covets it for his razor?

The poetic connection is one of those things that can't really be taught so much as pointed out. Every composer will have his unique method(s) of getting to it, from score to score and perhaps even from song to song. But it's a connection you must make.

For when it's in force, the music tells a good part of the tale. It conjures the universe and it evokes the specifics.

SONG PLACEMENT

The placement of a song within a scene defines 50 percent of its effectiveness, at a minimum.

The traditional philosophy goes: When the emotions become so large that speech isn't enough, you sing. Stephen Sondheim posed a new-age variation: When things get a little too tense to talk about, you sing.

Both or either can be *very* true, and often; but as self-contained axioms, both can also—sometimes—lead you to terrific songs that don't work within the dramatic context as well as you thought they might; because—again *sometimes,* and especially when you're trying to musicalize very richly written scenes—there can be more than one emotional or situational trigger, sometimes only seconds apart from one another. And sometimes the false lead is the line or phrase you're most attracted to as lyric fodder.

When all else fails, force yourself to let go of any preconceptions as to who should sing, what lines of dialogue inspire you, or the kind of song you thought you needed to round out the score. Examine the scene for two things: the place where dramatic tension *begins* and the place where it *ends.* This is frequently the span of the song, and marks the territory to be absorbed *into* song, because it tracks the central *event* of the scene. (In scenes that don't precisely comply with those markers, or have different needs—say, a set piece for your star, or the establishment of dramatic themes that will inform the action or the evening—an alternate approach may be to take stock of all the things you want the audience to pay attention to, focus on, and understand in a particular light. The overriding topic idea that acts as an umbrella for the others will tend to give your song its proper emphasis. For more on this, see the discussion of "God, That's Good!" in "Sticking to the Subject" later in this chapter.) The more you let these markers guide you toward song, the more you will find that the ultimate structure of the show and the programming of the score will shake down and refine themselves somewhat naturally—and ever more fleetly as you near the home stretch; there is something undeniably Zen and exhilarating about the process of letting the show "tell" you what it needs.

Inevitably, though, you will write songs that need to be replaced or reconsidered. That's part of exploring and learning your material. At times the wrong song will even demonstrate that a *structural problem* is at the root, and you and your librettist will find yourself "working backwards" to locate it.

One more thing about placement. In most cases, a song should not duplicate information we already know. If the audience is ahead of the song's function, the chances are it will be what's called a "stage wait" that attenuates narrative speed. (Love ballads are especially susceptible. Note that in most of the classic ones, the discovery of the emotion, and/or the *meaning* of the discovery to the character is contained *within the song*. The reason why these ballads move us so is because revelation and music *dovetail*.) What can be very tricky here is the manner in which the audience has learned the info that hurts your song. Sometimes you haven't point-blank come out and *told* them the information that neutralizes the effectiveness of the number. Sometimes the reveal is subtly implicit, through a character's prior behavior, or the assumed ramifications of a course of story action. Sometimes you'll discover you've tried to sing about something the audience doesn't *need* to know, an emotional or narrative transition that (unpleasant surprise!) *can be excised without the audience ever missing it!* Especially when your show's structure is still in flux, you can create a "security leak" and not even know you've done so. When a song's failure is utterly bewildering in every other respect, search keenly for the unintentional giveaway. Once it's found, the question then becomes whether you pull back on what you reveal earlier, drop the song, or go back to the structural drawing board before again *attempting* song. All three of these scenarios, and variations thereof, will play themselves out as you continue to write musicals.

SINGABILITY

Singability is linked to a number of things working in concert:

- Ease of pronunciation
- Ease of articulation
- Placement of vowel sounds and consonants to facilitate such ease
- Coordination of sound with range (e.g., the short *i* in *is* is a closed vowel sound that is hard to sustain on a held note, harder still on a high note, and produces an ugly sound)
- Regard for how the actor must use tongue, teeth, and breath. In a must-have Sondheim lecture transcript from the 1970s (see Appendix III at the end of this book), the composer-lyricist points out that in an early draft of "Getting Married Today," from *Company*, he began Amy's bullet-fast run-on aside to the audience with the phrase "Wait a sec." Upon consideration, he realized that the W required the actress to work her jaw, which would create a muscular tightness that would impede her being able to fire off the lyric at speed. He changed it to "Pardon me," because the simple plosive required only the use of the lips,

conserved the expenditure of air for the long phrase to boot, and allowed for the jaw to stay more relaxed through it all, because the kickoff could be accomplished without tension.

(Examine almost any patter song by a master lyricist of the American musical theatre; and invite Noël Coward along for good measure. Honoring the rhythmic scan, and without going to absurd extremes, try to say the words so quickly that you become tongue-tied. Chances are you won't be able to. The choice and juxtaposition of consonants and vowels has to be *that* meticulous.)

COMPREHENSIBILITY

From the same Sondheim lecture: "Lyrics go with music and music is very rich, in my opinion the richest form of art. It's also abstract and does very strange things to your emotions, so not only do you have that going, but you also have lights, costumes, scenery, characters, performers. There's a great deal to hear and get. Lyrics therefore have to be underwritten. They have to be very simple in essence. That doesn't mean you can't do convoluted lyrics, but essentially the thought is what counts and you have to stretch out enough so that the listener has a fair chance to get it. Many lyrics suffer from being much too packed."

STICKING TO THE SUBJECT

An oft-cited principle is that any given song must be about one thing and one thing only. This is actually a provocative dictum, because the more sophisticated and accomplished the songwriter, the more sophisticated the application can be.

In its simplest manifestation, any song you write must hew to only one subject or thesis and its development. When Pippin sings "Corner of the Sky," the topic is solely his desire to find his place in life. When Amy sings "Getting Married Today," the topic is solely her wild ambivalence about the coming nuptials, and the church choir and Paul's vow of devotion (which occur between verses) only serve to heighten that.

However—take a number like "God, That's Good" from *Sweeney Todd*. Overall it really *is* about one thing: establishing the success Mrs. Lovett and Sweeney have had with the pie shop since he's begun his murder spree with her complicity. But look what it includes: Tobias's invitation to potential customers; Mrs. Lovett's tending to the customers as they swoon over the meat pies; the arrival of Sweeney's new barber chair for greater ease of corpse disposal; the *testing* of the barber chair by Todd and Lovett. The structural secret though, is again, that *everything within the song* feeds and informs the rising good fortunes of our dark hero and his equally dark love-besotted muse—and each subtopic has *its own discrete module of music,* so that we're never disoriented by a shift in perspective. But perspective is the only thing that *does* shift. The main event of the song, the principle subject, obtains throughout.

PROPER ACCENT / FLAWLESS SCAN / PERFECT RHYME

Music and lyrics also need to work in concert toward the approximation of natural-sounding speech; even when the diction is poetic or stylized, the audience needs to maintain the fabled "suspension of disbelief" that allows for the illusion of utterances occurring naturally and spontaneously in song. This requires the rhetoric of the lyric—the places where the emphases and accents naturally rise and fall, not only in multisyllabic words, but in full phrases, and the placement of periods and commas—to be in impeccable sync with the music. And vice versa.

Perversely, my favorite musical is Edwards and Stone's *1776*—perversely because it is full of distracting lyric violations, most of them having to do with exactly the subject of natural emphasis. In John Adams' first song, "Piddle, Twiddle and Resolve" he complains to God about the Continental Congress and opens his protest with this (the italics are mine, to show where the principal accents fall):

> I DO BELIEVE YOU'VE LAID A CURSE ON
> NORTH AMERICA.
> A CURSE THAT WE HERE NOW REHEARSE IN
> PHILADELPHIA.

The energy and enthusiasm with which the composer-lyricist Sherman Edwards brings vital life to the play's historical figures and subject matter, plus his laser-sharp subject focus, gives you an excuse to be forgiving. And after a while, some ears are. But I don't think there's anyone who doesn't inwardly cringe *upon first listening* at the attempt to contort a rhyme out of AmeriCA and PhiladelphiYA. The natural accents are, of course, a-MEH-rica and philaDELphia. Which rhyme, respectively, with esoTErica and no existing word, but for the sake of argument, SELFia. (The Whitfield rhyming dictionary cites didelphia, monodelphia and polyadelphia, but these are not rhymes; they are rather identities, because the consonant starting the stress syllable does not change. Identities have their legitimate use in verbatim repetition of a line, for rhetorical emphasis—but under precious few other circumstances is an identity a proper or craft-legitimate substitute for a rhyme.) Nor is there good reason for the inclusion of the word *North,* save to preserve the run of sixteenth notes. It's obvious padding. (Even the word *do* is suspect, though colloquial usage justifies "I do believe" as a legitimate phrase.) The authentic utterance would be: "I [do] believe you've laid a curse on America," since Adams' concern is not the continent, but the particular country within it.[4]

Another place where Edwards commits what is perhaps the most *common* lyric infraction is in Martha Jefferson's song "He Plays the Violin," where he forces an EE rhyme by misaccenting a multisyllabic word:

WHEN HEAVEN CALLS TO *ME,*
SING ME NO SAD ELE*GY.*

---

4. In the aftermath of writing these words, I had to seek permission to quote the lyrics, and made the email acquaintance of Keith Edwards, Sherman's son, who oversees such matters. We got into a friendly (and quite lively) debate, in which he revealed that his father's technique choices were entirely intentional. I found the explanation so fascinating, and such a credible excuse for why the score hangs together so well in spite of what I'd cite as craft lapses, that I offered to present it in this footnote, toward a fully balanced view. For while rigorous craft should almost always be the rule, conscious choice toward specific effect can, used judiciously, justify legitimate exception. Here's what Keith wrote:

"Yes, craft is craft—and *1776's* lyrics follow the rules of a craft. What I think you overlook is that the show often follows the comedic rules, the craft, of VAUDEVILLE. When you open a show about the founding fathers with a lawyer joke, that's Vaudeville. When you have the founding fathers misuse the accents on simple words just to create a rhyme within a song, that is not poor craftmanship . . . it is good Vaudeville. When Dan Quayle spells potato 'potatoe'—that's funny. Sherman Edwards learned to play piano sitting on his mother Rachael's lap while she played for Eddie Cantor on stage. Sherman's roots came from Vaudeville.

"Perhaps you might ponder the possibility that the lyric works for the show because its comedic value serves as a foil for a book that often had to be serious . . . This explains the uncanny balance between the score's Vaudevillian humor and the book's serious events."

Indeed, one can find other pointed examples of craft violation serving stylistic nuance in the literature. In *Assassins,* Sondheim is clearly delivering a gloss on American folk song style when, in "The Ballad of Czolgosz" (pronounced CHOLE-gosh) he writes: "CZOLGOSZ, / WORKING MAN, / BORN IN THE MIDDLE OF MICHIGAN . . . "

The properly accented word, of course, is *eh*-legy, which rhymes, again, for the sake of argument, with *smellegy* and *hellegy*. Not with *Meee*.

Ironically, the score also contains an entire song whose conceit is a *celebration* of the misaccent infraction, *as well as* the use of identity rather than rhyme, *but one in which the violations are entirely proper;* because said celebration utterly informs character, to the point of using a technical identity to reinforce a *personal* identity. The song, "The Lees of Old Virginia" is sung by the proud and cocksure delegate Richard Henry Lee, trumpeting the sturdy reliability of his family line, and all the ways in which the Lees have distinguished themselves. (All the italics here belong to the lyricist.)

LEE
Y'SEE IT'S
HERE A LEE,
THERE A LEE,
EVERYWHERE A LEE, A LEE!

FRANKLIN and LEE, alternating
SOCIAL—
              —LEE!

POLITICAL—
              —LEE!

FINANCIAL—
              —LEE!

NATURAL—
              —LEE!

*I*NTERNAL—
              —LEE!

*E*XTERNAL—
              —LEE!

*F*RATERNAL—
              —LEE!

*E*TERNAL—
              —LEE!

The second time this *Lee* refrain appears, the character is rattling off the notable members of his illustrious family. And note how fresh and funny and right the lyric is when the identity is finally abandoned for this refrain's first true rhyme.

                              LEE
                    LOOK OUT! THERE'S
                    ARTHUR LEE!
                    BOBBY LEE . . . AN'
                    GENERAL "LIGHTHORSE" HARRY LEE!
                    JESSE LEE!
                    WILLIE LEE!

                          FRANKLIN
                    AND RICHARD H.—

                              LEE
                    THAT'S ME!!

Interestingly, you *can* legitimize a *contrived* (as opposed to a *forced*) EE rhyme by playing fair with natural accents. Stephen Sondheim may not have invented the technique, but I think its free use in the last few decades might be traceable to this quatrain from 1979's *Sweeney Todd* (italics mine, to emphasize the musical stress):

                    SWING YOUR *RAZOR WIDE,* SWEENEY!
                    HOLD IT *TO* THE *SKIES.*
                    FREELY FLOWS THE *BLOOD* OF *THOSE* WHO
                    MORALIZE.

The rhyming IZEs land on sustained notes, but the stress falls differently. *Skies* lands on the first beat of its bar—but *moralize* is set as an eighth-note triplet, whose first syllable lands on the first beat of *its* bar. The rhyme satisfies while never jerking the ear to accommodate an unnatural flow.

MORE ON RHYME

Sondheim:

You try to make your rhyming seem fresh but inevitable, and you try for surprise but not so wrenchingly that the listener loses the sense of the line. . . . The true function of the rhyme is to point up the word that rhymes—if you don't want that word to be the most important in the line, don't rhyme it. Also, rhyme helps shape the music, it helps the listener hear what the shape of the music is. Inner rhymes, which are fun to work out if you have a puzzle mind, have one function, which is to speed the line along. . . .

[Another] function of rhyme is that it shows intelligence and a controlled state of mind. The run-on sections of the bride number "Getting Married Today," in *Company* were purposely without rhyme. If they did contain rhyme, she would not have been hysterical and would have been in greater control. For the songs for the character of Fredrik, the lawyer in *A Little Night Music*, however, I used heavy rhyming because he is a man who rationalizes everything and does a lot of thinking.

Maury Yeston, in his classes, has made the point that when a score flagrantly abandons proper rhyme and accent, it sends an unintended message to the audience that wit will not be a feature of the evening, and because of that they stop listening carefully, having just been "told" that language will not matter. Audiences do thus pick up *dozens* of subliminal signals, informing their responses and nonresponses, and that can never be underestimated. As my friend actor Daniel Marcus has said, "Audiences are not only smarter than *you* think they are . . . they're smarter than *they* think they are."

FRESH IMAGERY

Imagery is all-important, because it helps anchor meaning while (conversely) speeding the lyric along; the right image, or images, creates an astonishingly powerful shorthand. Let's consider again Stephen Schwartz's "Corner of the Sky" (an AB or Verse-Chorus song, by the way):

> EVERYTHING HAS ITS SEASON,
> EVERYTHING HAS ITS TIME.
> SHOW ME A REASON
> AND I'LL SOON SHOW YOU A RHYME.
> CATS FIT ON THE WINDOWSILL,
> CHILDREN FIT IN THE SNOW.
> WHY DO I FEEL I DON'T FIT IN
> ANYWHERE I GO?

> RIVERS BELONG WHERE THEY CAN RAMBLE,
> EAGLES BELONG WHERE THEY CAN FLY.
> I'VE GOT TO BE WHERE MY SPIRIT CAN RUN FREE.
> GOTTA FIND MY CORNER OF THE SKY.

This not only sets up, neatly and concisely, the hero's quest, but gives us a sense of his character through the metaphors and similes that matter to him. True, the opening subject line is a familiar sentiment, and the reason/rhyme couplet is hardly fresh—but they earn their keep by stating the universally identification-worthy thesis and providing a context for its explication: "Cats fit on the windowsill / Children fit in the snow." Could anything be more evocative? Even the basic metaphor: Pippin sees his place in the world as his corner of the sky. Clearly he cannot stand the notion of being earthbound.

SUBTEXT

Subtext is among the most popular buzzwords applied to musical theatre lyrics. But it is also among your most valuable tools. Subtext is what gives the lyric—and by extension the character(s) singing—depth, complexity, and humanity that transcend the broad strokes and economy of song. Subtext is what's going on *behind* the words. A few examples:

In "Poor Jud Is Dead" from *Oklahoma!* Curly's imagining of the redemptive funeral Jud might have is phrased with impeccable care. The not-too-bright Jud thinks he's being respected, but we in the audience recognize it for the put-down that it is, in canny lines like "His fingernails have never been so clean."

In *Follies,* Ben Stone sings of "The Road You Didn't Take" and a life in which it "never comes to mind," where "One has regrets which one forgets." Meanwhile the insistence of the lyric, and the dissonance of the music, tell us that he's protesting too much, and is, in fact, *obsessed* with the past.

In *Fiddler on the Roof,* only half the fun is seeing the fantastic nightmare the dairyman describes in "Tevye's Dream." The other half is knowing that it's an elaborate ruse to make his wife go along with their daughter Tzeitl marrying Motel the poor, young tailor, whom she loves, rather than Lazar Wolf the old, rich butcher, whom she doesn't.

The famous, oft-cited example is "Some People" in *Gypsy.* It's a powerful statement of self and philosophy, all right . . . but the only reason Mama Rose takes the trouble to sing it is because she's trying to convince her father to let her hock his prized plaque, so she can continue to finance her kids' vaudeville careers. And speaking of subtext, unarticulated right up until "Rose's Turn" is the nonetheless clear notion that Rose is trying to live vicariously, through her kids, the career in showbiz she herself never had.

Oscar Hammerstein II often wrote what he called the "almost" love song, at a point in the story too early for the characters to acknowledge their feelings out loud, and kept romantic tension going with theses like, "*If* I Loved You," and "*People Will Say* We're in Love."

There are literally hundreds of classic examples, and not incidentally, they constitute a good deal of what distinguishes the artful American musical from the artless Euro, which so often favors "on the nose" declamation. It's much more effective to have the audience *intuit* an emotion or an objective than to simply *tell* them, because that intuition is what engages emotional involvement (not to mention a richer use of language and character) and maintains suspense.

BUTTON, BUTTON . . .

Knowing how to end a number properly (and appropriately) is as important as knowing how to structure and sustain one.

When seeking applause, you apply what's called a "button." Essentially this is an emphasized musical period that returns to the tonic for musical closure—while also providing psychological and perceptual closure for the dramatic beat. A button tends to appear as a rhythmic figure that "concludes" the accompaniment vamp or feel; a brief postscript that puts a final flip on a motive derived from the tune; or a simple, accented beat, bang, pluck, chord, or otherwise *articulated* "hit."

Legendarily innovative orchestrator Jonathan Tunick talks amusingly of what he considers the three most commonly applied generic buttons, which he has dubbed *Nina, Twink,* and *Dah-yumph.*

- The first ends an energetic, up-tempo number:

    YUP-datup-datup,
    YUP-datup-datup,
    YUP-datup-datup dah!
    NINA!

- The second ends a ballad:

    IIIIIIIIII . . .
    Loooooooooove . . .
    Youuuuuuuuuuu.

    (*twink*)

- The third ends a big, brassy ascending-note fanfare that *ritards* and crescendos toward a held chord, when you're trying to milk

applause ("from a number that doesn't really work," Tunick likes
to archly add); generally the last two melody notes describe a slur
or *glissando* from a high- or middle-range note to the single or
double octave below:

Dum-beedledum-dum
Bah
Bah
Bah
Bah
DAHHHHHHHH—
yumph!!!

These, of course, are among the primary clichés, because of their universally comprehended *finality*—but there are many and perhaps infi-
nite ways to vary the expected stew, if you like. The trick, in all instances,
is to render your button in a way that is stylistically, dramatically correct— plus gratifyingly and utterly unambiguous. It has to convey the
unequivocal message: *Applaud here!*

Should a button fail to elicit the desired applause, and you've eliminated the song itself as the problem, there is a list of variables to consider,
and you'll find them at the end of this chapter.

That said, there is one *other* question to be considered where buttons
are concerned.

Should the number button for applause at all?

Will the applause be at cost to dramatic tension that should be sustained until a more resonant, more significant point? Does the number's
content reflect closure, or does it leave the character unresolved? Does
the number's button ask the audience to approve a character or character
choice they find unsettling? Would the button be less powerful than a
delicate silence? Is the number threaded through, or punctuating, a
longer sequence in which it is reprised for higher stakes (and energy?)
each time—and if so, would it be better to save applause until the last
incarnation of the number definitively, finally *concludes?*

If any of the above (or variations) apply, you may find that you need to
"cheat out" applause by making sure the audience *never* gets that clear
signal to start clapping. Since audiences, through conditioning, are often
poised to applaud, the choice to "cheat out" must be rendered in a manner just as unambiguous, so that the audience (subconsciously, because

you don't want them to *think* about the ritual they're not performing) is led *away* from the desire to applaud.

Among the standard methods of to doing so are

- to keep instrumental music vamping or chording, usually without conclusive harmonic resolution, as the final vocal note comes to its end, bring in dialogue *over* that instrumental extension, and begin a new scene before the music concludes or fades out. (See "The Road You Didn't Take" from *Follies*.)
- to end without resolving the music—thus mirroring an unresolved thought or unanswered question. (See "Is Anybody There?" from *1776*.)
- to cut music short. (See Don Quixote's death near the end of *Man of La Mancha*; or the end of "Mountain Town" in the film *South Park: Bigger, Longer and Uncut*—not to be confused with the ending on the film's soundtrack album, for which a button was added.)
- to interrupt the expectation of a celebratory button with tragedy. (See the wedding dance, near the end of Act One in *Fiddler on the Roof*.) Or a new plot development that brings its own new *musical* interruption. (See Anthony's entrance breaking into the end of "Pretty Women" in *Sweeney Todd*.)

And, as with the creation of buttons, the engineering of "cheats" can be likewise prodigious and varied.

Sometimes—though less frequently—the decision to use a button or eschew it can be controversial:

When the original 1979 production of *Sweeney Todd* was in early previews, Todd's "Epiphany"—the number in which he finally flips into full-tilt madness, anticipates his coming killing spree, and exults, "But the work waits! I'm alive at last! And I'm full of joy!"—the final vocal note was a violation of mental peace, held over a hard, brass chord which released into an eerie high-string dissonance . . . which was suspended like hovering death, while Sweeney stood there, razor high and breathing hard . . . until Mrs. Lovett's cautious intrusion.

By the time the show opened, "Epiphany" buttoned with the brass chord held just long enough for a quick timpani roll, leading to a simultaneous timpani-and-brass hit. It got its applause, with expert *Dah-yumph*-variant efficiency (which may be no coincidence, as Jonathan Tunick orchestrated the score); but during the previews between, while the creative team were experimenting, finding the way to button a number not fundamentally *built* to do so was not an instant process, and the intermediate results left the audience confused. Were they meant to approve Sweeney's decision? Acknowledge the performer's accomplishment and break with verisimilitude? Applause was at first tepid and tentative.

I later learned that Sondheim had not been in favor of the button, precisely because of the mixed and antidramatic agenda it seemed to have. But a colleague not on the creative team had put the bug in director Hal Prince's ear, and the ensuing disagreement was unpleasant enough that Sondheim thought it best to give in.

But you'll notice the unbuttoned version was preserved on the original cast album—and indeed, too, in several subsequent productions of note—most prominently the widely emulated vest-pocket, cast-of-fourteen "reduction" devised by director Susan Schulman, which transferred from off-Broadway's York Theatre to Broadway's Circle in the Square a decade later—"Epiphany" has been performed *sans* button.

ISN'T IT A (SELF) PITY?

There is a popular rule of lyric craft that advises you never to write a song of self-pity (except in comedy). The rationale is that the audience is more willing to supply pity for a character trying to *stoically tough out* a difficult situation than it is to empathize with one *complaining* about his or her situation.

But since self-pity is very often a powerful tool of unmusicalized drama (as well as comedy) when used judiciously, I don't think the normal caution fully explains the phenomenon of audiences resisting, or even tuning out, self-pitying songs. On closer examination, there's something *additionally* at work endemic to musicals specifically.

Active characters need, even in moments of reflection, to *remain* in action—*thinking* forward if not literally *moving* forward. Self-pity is a look backwards, and by definition puts the character in suspended animation. It isn't so much the self-pity that audiences resist, but rather the condition of stasis. The dramatic language of musical theatre, remember, is one of shorthand and compression. If a situation is bad for a character, the audience *knows* it's bad, and don't need reminding. They're interested in what/how the character is planning to, or *going* to, do about it, or adjust to it.

Even if we look at arguably the most extreme example in the canon, Fosca from Sondheim and Lapine's *Passion*—indeed, she wallows in self-pity. But never to us. Only to Giorgio and only in pursuit of his affections. Perversely, self-pity *is among her active tools.*

Now there's a "back door" rule about self-pity—that it's permissible on occasion *if it's earned.* Certainly one could argue that in Wasserman, Darion, and Leigh's *Man of La Mancha,* when the whore Aldonza sings the song named for her, railing at Don Quixote for giving her false hope, and cataloguing the miseries of her life, she has earned her tirade. After all, by acceding to his philosophy of nobility, she has instigated her own gang rape by the Muleteers.

But examine even *that* moment carefully. It isn't the self-pity that holds our interest; it's Aldonza's enraged attempt to shock Quixote, to get a rise out of him ("Can't you see what your gentle insanities do to me?"); the more he stands firm and implacable, the more her fury grows. Self-pity is a weapon here, and there is a real, present, active contest of wills going on.

Which brings us to self-pity within comedy . . .

I think even here, if you examine most self-pity moments, you'll see that there's almost always something *active* fueling the proceedings, even if only implicitly. When Miss Hannigan sings "Little Girls" in Meehan, Strouse, and Charnin's *Annie,* we've just met her and she's telling us something we don't know yet, at least not fully, which is the endless treadmill on which she sees herself, overseeing her charges in the orphanage. And because she's so flagrant and inappropriate about it, we know she's our villain. And because she expresses her frustration at the top, the song functions as an "I Want" number. She wants *out,* and just as clearly, from her fantasies about being rid of the little darlings, she's primed to do something about it at the soonest opportunity. The self-pity isn't stasis at all; it's her personal motivator.

The most common use of self-pity in comedy, however, is as a tool for solving a problem. Look at the example from *Avenue Q* citied earlier. Brian and Kate Monster are in active pursuit of their goals; they just haven't reached them yet and find themselves bemused by that. (And again, note the placement. We're just at the top of the show, just meeting the characters, and those brief verses are backstory essences; we're not going over old ground.)

Here's another, "Doctor Lucy" from the late Clark Gesner's *You're a Good Man, Charlie Brown.* Charlie Brown is seated at Lucy's Psychiatric Health Booth.

CHARLIE BROWN
I'M NOT VERY HANDSOME OR CLEVER OR
    LUCID.
I'VE ALWAYS BEEN STUPID AT SPELLING AND
    NUMBERS.
I'VE NEVER BEEN MUCH PLAYING FOOTBALL,
    OR BASEBALL,
OR STICKBALL, OR CHECKERS, OR MARBLES, OR
    PING-PONG.
I'M USUALLY AWFUL AT PARTIES AND DANCES.
I STAND LIKE A STICK, OR I COUGH, OR I
    LAUGH.
OR I DON'T BRING A PRESENT,
OR I SPILL THE ICE CREAM,
OR I GET SO DEPRESSED THAT I STAND AND I
    SCREAM,
"OH, HOW COULD THERE POSSIBLY BE
ONE SMALL PERSON AS
THOROUGHLY, TOTALLY, UTTERLY . . . BLAH
AS ME?"

And why do we love him for this?
The setting.
He's at the psychiatrist's office. Such as it is.
He's not there to wallow.
As with anyone who goes into therapy, he's being courageous, exposing his weaknesses and trying to get to the bottom of them.
He's there to solve a problem.
When *ostensible* self-pity works, somewhere, somehow, directly or implicitly, it's covering new ground and it's *active!*

ED'S FIFTEEN

Ed Kleban, renowned lyricist of *A Chorus Line,* and posthumous composer-lyricist of the show about his life, *A Class Act,* had a number of rules for musical dramatists to live by.

Among the most memorable was what he called The Rule of Two: "Never discuss the show within a two-block radius of the theatre," because the odds of being *overheard* by someone *involved* were, in his opinion, too great.

He argued The Rule of Ten to BMI management in order to save its Musical Theatre Workshop, imperiled in the wake of founder-teacher Lehman Engel's death, when corporate honchos suggested that the program hadn't produced enough alumni of note: "It takes a doctor, a lawyer, an engineer or any such professional ten years of training, apprenticeship, and mistake-making to learn his craft and produce notable results—why should it be any less true for a writer?"

And then there was The Rule of Twenty-Four: "If you turn your back on a musical in rehearsal for twenty-four hours, you'll return to find the ship has begun sailing in another direction."

A corollary to his rules was his famous List of Fifteen. That is, the list of fifteen things that can be wrong with a song onstage *after you've ruled out the possibility that the song itself is at fault.* And they are:

1. **Tempo.** Is it too fast to be understood, too slow to build the proper energy?
2. **Orchestration.** Is the arrangement so busy as to be distracting; so spare as to shortchange the ambiance?
3. **Lighting.** Can you see it properly?
4. **Costume.** Is the stage picture appropriate?
5. **Character who sings it.** Do we care about this person? Can the sentiment possibly be expressed better by another?
6. **The setup.** Are we properly prepared for the number?
7. **Placement in the score.** Does the number appear too late (after we know what it tells us) or too soon (before we're ready to absorb it)? [See "Song Placement" earlier in the chapter.]
8. **Location on stage it's sung from.** Is it being properly featured? Is it given the focus it deserves?
9. **Key.** Is it too high or too low to be effective? In general? In the actor's particular range?
10. **The set.** Is the song in its proper environment?
11. **The staging.** In most cases, it is the *lyric* that should be staged, and not *up*staged by irrelevant business.
12. **Minor lyric changes vs. major music changes.** Are the revisions complementing each other, or has an imbalance been created?
13. **The intro.** Is the number beginning properly?
14. **The button.** Is the number *ending* properly? Is the music making the audience feel gratified at the song's completion? Does the staging provide the *right* kind of emphatic punctuation to make the audience feel secure about applauding?

15. **The actor.** Ed qualified this as "the last possible source of the problem," probably to dissuade defensive writers from reflexively using it as a convenient excuse, but indeed, the wrong actor can destroy a number—*any* number.

It's a good list to keep in mind during rehearsals, and one of the greatest gifts Ed could have left aspiring, and even veteran, musical dramatists. Because even though you have to be crazy to do this for a living, it's a blessing to remember that *sometimes* you're not *that* crazy. . . .

THE SECOND-BEST SOLUTION

As a corollary to Ed's list, let me alert you to one other possible problem.

We often get in our own way when we write for specific performers.

I'm not saying don't do it—in fact, it's often *mandatory* that you do it—not only in an applicable professional circumstance, but also to prime the creative pump. Nothing helps specificity like having a precise vocal quality, range, technique, and persona to use as a model. It's even more gratifying when the person in your head is actually the person who performs the song or the role.

But when the talents of that actor—the talents you're exploiting for virtuoso effect—are so specific as to reduce, or preclude, the chances of *another* actor doing as well, it's good to have a backup version (or at least a backup *concept*) ready—one that will still satisfy the needs of the dramatic moment and your needs as an author. Among the worst environments to create for an actor is one in which she senses that she's living in the shadow of a better memory; among the worst to create for yourself is that moment in which you cringe a bit inside, because the actor can't quite deliver what you've written and never will, and you feel some absurdly purist obligation to "bear up" and hope against hope. So be realistic:

If the high note (or the sequence of notes providing its musical context), the key, the tongue-twisting dexterity—*whatever* the choice—should be technically beyond the reach of an otherwise able performer, ask yourself what's lost if you concede the moment to something less showy. If the answer is "What the audience doesn't know won't hurt them"—or you, or the show, or the story, or the actor—then you have no practical (or even compellingly artistic) reason to be intractable.

Your compromise doesn't have to be the best moment in the world—merely the best one you can make it and still live with it.

Never kid yourself about the difficulty level of your material. What may seem easy and straightforward to you, because you understand it organically and internally, may remain perpetually elusive to someone trying to work it from the outside in. Not all actors—and I mean even some awfully good ones—are equally or optimally intuitive. There's no reason to compromise *unduly* or even *routinely*—but there's every reason to keep an open mind.

The second-best solution is often your first best choice.

SECTION THREE: **PRACTICAL APPLICATION**

6

CHAPTER

The Spirit of the Thing
or:
Adaptation

ONE WAY OR ANOTHER—AT ONE TIME OR ANOTHER—WE ALL break the cardinal rule of adaptation. Sometimes it's broken due to the limits of our personal vision as writers; sometimes it's broken due to the limits of *others*, creating political pressures that slowly *erode* our vision. Most times, if we're lucky, we manage not to break it at all, or only briefly as we find our way, before getting back on track. But the breaking of this rule is, I think, among the two or three most common reasons why musicals fail. And the rule is this:

Never lose sight of the essential qualities that make your source material attractive to begin with.

The only reason to adapt a work is to enhance and elevate the compelling things it already contains.

That said, there's a curious paradox. The rule cannot be taken *literally* any more than it can be taken *lightly*. Because it exists side-by-side with *this* provocative truth: you (and your collaborators) are often the ones to decide what those "essential qualities" and "compelling things" are. In certain instances you can extrapolate them wholesale or even make them up. That depends upon the characteristics of the source property, what it gives you to work with, the type of musical it inspires, and your intentions.

THE SKILL AND THE TRICK

Over 90 percent of the time, though, you will find that even the most *liberal* adaptations honor the *spirit* of the source material—and that the more faithful adaptations honor texture, diction, and tone as well.

The *skill* is to properly identify those characteristics.

The *trick* is to hold onto them throughout the months, sometimes years, of your show's gestation.

I won't address the *trick* in detail because that's often a wholly subjective affair about which one can draw no general conclusions. Every production situation is unique—the human factor changes, even if the lessons of history do not—and usually requires a balancing act between artistic and political concerns. The *trick* depends largely upon the sharpness of your self-critical eye and ear as your show develops—combined with how much muscle and/or willingness you have to draw a line in the sand when the quality *or even the very existence* of the piece is threatened by one or another of the power brokers who come on board to make full production a reality.

But the *skill* is what gives you maximum ammo and your musical its strength and its spine. And the greater the *skill*—usually—the better your odds of pulling off the *trick*.

Let's consider several different types of source material:

Trash and Pulp

If you're adapting from a source that is poorly or "trashily" conceived, the compelling elements may be as large as the basic structure—e.g., the 1961 Roger Corman film *Little Shop of Horrors*—and as small as the basic character iconography—e.g., the 1910 Gaston Leroux penny dreadful *The Phantom of the Opera*.

Indeed, the respective Webber-Hart, Yeston-Kopit, and Spencer-Barron versions of *Phantom* tell three entirely different stories—stories equally distinct from the novel—because faithfulness to the book is simply impossible. The Leroux structure is a haphazard mess, the text a rough read, *its sole strength the central image of the beautiful soprano and her deformed mentor.* Every adaptation, be it musical or cinematic, has devised its own rationale to explain it. Meanwhile, the Ashman-Menken *Little Shop* maintains a remarkable respect for Charles B. Griffith's original screenplay in attitude, characterization, and delivery.

Pix and Lit

If you're adapting from a work that has deeper literary, cinematic, or thematic merit, the bar is raised and the ante is upped. Pieces like this tend to resonate in uniquely essential ways, and however you treat that essence, be it update (*Romeo and Juliet* into *West Side Story*) or straightforward reinterpretation (*Kiss of the Spider Woman*), the essence—the place where style, tone, and humanism merge to create a visceral response—has to be honored. And *felt*.

Bear in mind too that a highly popular, classic, precedent-setting or archetype-defining work is not *always*, but *often* possessed of what I call "organic integrity": a philosophical reason for its own existence—a palpable "soul," as it were—that will attach itself to any adaptive incarnation, *whether you want it to or not*.

If your adaptation taps into that soul—and maintains it healthily throughout the development process, such that the spirit of the piece remains always well represented—you may well ironically find yourself being lauded for faithfulness, *even if you have made sweeping changes in structure, characterization, and plot!* To paraphrase Billy Crystal's Fernando character, it's more important for your musical to *feel* faithful than to *be* faithful.

If, however, your adaptation *contradicts* that soul, the audience will *always* sense the disparity, *even if they're not familiar with the source material*.

Here's an example:

Franz Werfl's 1944 play, *Jacobowsky and the Colonel*—a story of two Poles, an anti-Semitic aristocrat and a humble, resourceful Jew, obliged to escape from the Nazis in the same car—is a sincere "buddy" comedy-drama. Core to its existence are the themes of heterosexual male bonding, overcoming prejudice, and achieving survival against a war-torn background.

Musicalized in 1979 as *The Grand Tour* by Jerry Herman (score) and Michael Stewart and Mark Bramble (book), it became an old-fashioned tuner—some lovely songs, but its musical palette indistinguishable from that of *Mame* or *Hello, Dolly!*, bereft of real threat (chorus-boy Nazis), and conspicuously without an authentic sense of buddy-ness between its two leads, the cartoonishly disparate Joel Grey and Ron Holgate (compare this casting to the more humanly disparate Danny Kaye and Curt Jürgens in the nonmusical film version, *Me and the Colonel*). It was restructured to center on a romantic triangle between the two men and a young French woman (played by powerhouse belter Florence Lacey, arguably Broadway's best *Evita* but no willow).

The treatment simply feels at odds with the tale. The title itself suggests where the authors go wrong—since when is a flight for your life a sightseeing excursion? The authors simply didn't "get" the piece—and thus the piece resisted them.

And here's a postscript from Herman's own autobiography, *Showtune.* When Michael Stewart *first approached him* about the project, Herman's response was, "That's a lovely play and it will probably make a very interesting musical. But I really don't want to do a musical about some man who is running from the Nazis. I would rather do something with showgirls." He confesses openly to the reader that "I never had a passion for the piece and I think it shows. When you have true love for something and go at it with passion, it always shows in the work."

Midlist and Obscuranta

You have more leeway to experiment with source material that is obscure, or that at least hovers safely below the radar of significant media visibility. A property from this vast well can present you with a fine idea or basic storyline that smart musicalization can only improve. Such a piece may not have so durable a soul as discussed in the section above, and in fact, may be a very mutable vessel *waiting for the soul you pour into it.*

For example, whereas Lynn Ahrens and Stephen Flaherty were obligated to somehow faithfully render E. L. Doctorow's *Ragtime,* a signature work of American fiction, they were not so obligated with the source of their first produced musical, *Lucky Stiff.*

That one, musicalized as a contemporary romantic farce whose main characters are distinctly American, was based on a slim comic caper period novel, *The Man Who Broke the Bank at Monte Carlo.* But that novel is set early in the twentieth century, and features a hero who, like its nevermore-than-midlist, multigenre author, Michael Butterworth, is British.

What such minor works provide are the inspirations, devices, notions, and conceits that let you create a universe beholden only to your own muse—yet one with a basic architecture already in place, a skeletal foundation upon which to build.

Not for nothing did Oscar Hammerstein II advise that the best projects to adapt are those that *almost* work. As a corollary to that I'd add: or those that seem to scream out for musical elevation—that seem *made* to be transformed.

Conversely, a piece that is *itself* transcendent is often only *diminished* by musicalization: that's why *Cyrano de Bergerac* has failed twice on Broadway and countless times regionally.

That said, you can, if you look diligently enough, find a low-profile but worthwhile property that both provides great raw material *and* bears inherent depth and integrity—even built-in marketability. (*The Fabulist,* currently in progress, by myself and Stephen Witkin, picked up several significant development awards, and in several smaller ways has had a serendipitous existence right from inception; but that's not just due to talent and luck: the high-concept *premise* of John Vornholt's paperback original novel—an epic fantasy-fable about Aesop—is as responsible for our good fortune as our treatment of it.)

These properties usually also have the advantage of being relatively easy and inexpensive to secure—and renew—theatrical rights to, if they're not already in the public domain. And that's your security. There comes a point in a musical dramatist's development where it's no longer useful to write learning exercises for strictly academic purposes. And that's the point where you have to be unsentimentally practical.

Indeed, what would you rather do? Option an "unknown" property to the tune of, oh, say, $1,000 for the first eighteen months, renewable for the same every year of the next three thereafter—a property that may well come along with the creator's enthusiasm . . . or spend eighteen months of costly effort pursuing a high-octane property only to learn that the rights holders don't think *you* have the octane, financially or career-wise, to merit it? Is it worth the wasted exploratory and speculative drafts of outlines, scenes, and songs? The time spent on tenterhooks waiting for a response? The merciless yanking around of your soul by the legal dogs on the other side?

You want to spend time doing work that you know will come to something—not worrying about whether you even have the right (or the rights) to work!

Pop and Icons

If you're adapting from the pop culture iconography of licensed, trademarked, or series characters (in musicals this most commonly tends toward comic book or comic strip characters, less frequently toward characters who are genre mainstays), you have perhaps the hardest adaptive challenge of all. Because it allows almost no margin for error, and precious little for reinvention.

Think about it: Traditionally, in musicals, main characters go on some kind of quest, or have some overarching goal that propels them through a rite of passage. They emerge at the end somehow changed for the experience, usually for the better.

However, the two most cherished qualities of classic genre and graphic-art characters are their familiarity and their *consistency*. They can become richer and more complex on the page or the screen, as lore gets added to canon and story builds upon story—but 98 percent of the time *they do not fundamentally change!*

Musicals about Sherlock Holmes have always been ill-advised because despite all the great detective's signature peccadilloes, he is at core an enigma, which defies singing from the heart and expressing true emotion. Indeed, his ability to obfuscate is key to his brilliance as an investigator. Violate any of this and you invoke the impatience—even the wrath—of an audience whose expectations have been, likewise, violated. Who begin to think (correctly) that *they* know the characters better than *you* do. (More recently, *Nick and Nora*—about the married sleuths from the *Thin Man* series—fell into this same trap. The Charleses having serious *marital problems???* Sacrilege!!!)

One of the reasons why the original 1968 off-Broadway version of *You're a Good Man, Charlie Brown* was so stunningly successful was that it was only marginally a book musical. Really it was a revue of songs and sketches that took Charlie Brown and the rest of the *Peanuts* gang through two typical days, one per act. Author-composer Clark Gesner's light, subtle touch was an ideal match for the gentle humor of Charles Schulz's strip, and the vignettes were themselves the theatrical equivalents of strips. By the same token, the 1999 Broadway revival of the show failed—just as stunningly—because it *refused* to honor the strip's gentility and subtlety. The score was reworked (not by Gesner, who had no control or say in the matter), the characters grossly exaggerated, and the humor rendered loud-fast-broad in a way that vulgarized and cheapened the franchise. With the exception of children, who took some solace and delight in the show's bright design and silliness, most audience members new to the show couldn't understand why anyone would want to revive anything so aggressively childish—and those who knew the show well tended to be irritated at the desecration.

Characters whose personalities and official mythos have been absorbed into the public consciousness are very powerful *without* you—affection for them, even intimacy *with* them, *walks in the door with your audience*—and the universal, emblematic popularity of these creations exists for good reason.

If you can't present them authentically, tread not on their ground.

YOU AND IT

The different types of adaptation thus considered, the correct match of your palette to the required tone of the piece is ultimately *everything*.

Is the story you're adapting, its characters and themes, a natural fit with your verbal and/or musical sensibility? If not "naturally" so, do you have an instinctive-enough affinity, or a rigorous-enough intellect, to make the stretch and *find* the place where it can *feel* natural? Can you *absorb* its signature style points into your own? Abe Burrows didn't use a line of Damon Runyon in his book for *Guys and Dolls*—a totally original tale inspired by bits of various short stories—but he made it sound as if it were lifted verbatim. He understood the *rhythm*—and he gave Runyon-savvy audiences the world they thought they knew.

In addition to considering the material's needs, consider your own strengths, weaknesses, predilections, and prejudices. No matter how much you may like a property, if its defining characteristics seem elusive—or, alternatively, if the defining characteristics are the thing you most want to change to make it fit within your wheelhouse—examine your motives. Be honest with yourself about what kind of adaptation you're doing . . . and how well the material will bear up under the chemical fusion of you and it.

Yes, the popular philosophy is a sound one: You must worship and love your source material—and then be willing to blast it to smithereens it in order to create a musical that works.

Never forget, though, the measure of your respect for the material lies not in how much or how little you change its particulars . . .

. . . it's in the nature, dignity and *spirit* of the reconstruction . . .

7

CHAPTER

The Bogus Condition
or:
Writer's Block

THERE IS NO SUCH THING AS WRITER'S BLOCK. NOT WHEN A musical with a decently developing foundation is under way.

There is emotional turmoil and personal mishegoss that can interfere with writing, to be sure; and certainly the need to juggle a pay-the-bills "civilian" job with limited creative time can sap one's energy and concentration—at least until you figure out how to prioritize and pace yourself. But allowing for the absence or the moderation or the mastery of such real-life distractions, and the presence of even mild professional-minded functionality, writer's block is a mythical malady borne of four quite real symptoms:

1. You don't have enough information.
2. The song or scene you're trying to write is resisting you because the underlying premise is false.
3. Something is intrinsically amiss with your story structure or your underlying theme, and in trying to accommodate the flaw, you're running up against its limitations.
4. What you're trying to write simply isn't good enough by your own standards, and your internal barometer is urging you to start again.

Learning to diagnose the symptoms is what gets you over the hump. To elaborate:

You don't have enough information. Means exactly what it says. You can't write about a *shtetl* under Cossack rule without researching Russia.

You can't attempt a 1930s light verse song pastiche without being conversant with the likes of Noël Coward and Cole Porter. You can't cogently outline a character's dramatic trajectory without knowing how his/her principle objective informs his/her progress through the play.

If you're not solving the problem, one of the first questions to ask yourself is *Do I actually know what I'm doing?*

The song or scene you're trying to write is resisting you because the underlying premise is false. Sometimes the internal logic of a song or scene is fighting the play's reality base, or even a reasonable tenet of human behavior. Examine the plot and/or the psychological premise upon which the scene or song is based. Strip away everything but a thumbnail description of what it's trying to accomplish. Within the fictional universe, is it credible? Do you believe it? If you could ask the character in all honesty, would s/he believe it? Or is it somehow tortured, attenuated, rationalized, contrived, implausible?

It's natural to want to overlook these questions, since most of us hate to have "wasted" energy on a false lead. But you have to ask them. For what's astonishing is the even more draining energy we can otherwise put into fooling ourselves.

Something is intrinsically amiss with your story structure or your underlying theme, and in trying to accommodate the flaw, you're running up against its limitations. To repeat something I said in Chapter 4: One of the most common, yet oh-so-subtle problems that can best a gestating musical is the point at which it shifts from what you *thought* it was about to what it's *really* about. The point where you feel painted into a corner, or as if nothing you write is quite good enough to put you over the top, is a terrific time to reexamine your musical and see if it hasn't grown into something else when you weren't looking.

When Stephen Witkin and I began writing our Aesop musical *The Fabulist*, we were certain it was a parable about learning to accept your own flawed humanity. The opening number, for a Greek chorus of fable animals, was called, fittingly enough, "They're Only Human," which was a light-hearted condemnation of the qualities that make people less noble than birds and beasts.

The number stayed in the show through two developmental readings; readings in which we discovered that plot points we considered major were not having their proper impact upon the audience. The most major of all concerned the way Aesop used his fables. As he explores his gift for them, he realizes they get him out of trouble, because they deal in metaphor and allow him to make harsh criticism of powerful people through entertaining stories that never precisely name names or point fingers. And late in the play his luck runs out when, angered by an injustice that affects him on a deep, personal level, Aesop *forgets* to concoct a fable and criticizes directly: a lapse that leads to his being framed, arrested, and facing a death sentence.

In both of the first two readings, the "crime" of direct criticism played as a dramatic afterthought, and the "punishment" meted out for it seemed arbitrary and whimsical. Yet it was the very crux of the denouement. In truth, this had been a source of debate between Stephen Witkin and me. In the denouement, our musical pretty much echoed the lovely novel by John Vornholt on which it is based—and in the novel the denouement had felt to me something of a throwaway, too. But Stephen insisted that it was important and did not want to reinvent that part of the story.

And in the aftermath of the second reading—in that ideal downtime, when I had absorbed the notes I'd been given, there was no immediate deadline, and things were quietly perking in the back of my mind—I had a sudden epiphany.

If that plot point of the denouement was so goddamn important, I reasoned, then everything in the play had to lead up to it—*point* to it. Which meant the very theme of the play had to focus on it and prepare us to understand its significance. "They're Only Human" was therefore the wrong opening number. And if it was the wrong opening, we were articulating the wrong dramatic theme.

I dropped my preconceptions and affections for existing parts of the score and traced the events and elements and concepts we were trying to highlight. And I threw Stephen for a temporary but profound loop by announcing: "The show is not about foibles and the endurance of the human spirit in spite of them. The show is about the nature of truth: how it's told and to whom and to what consequence." Not incidentally, that shift also threw the function of fables and Aesop's world-culture pervasiveness into high relief right at the start.

I wrote a number called "You Can Always Find a Fable," in which the animals set up the premise of fable as useful metaphor in difficult situations, and imply, without giving away the ending, that the very man they're here to honor had a fateful day when he forgot his own best strategy.

The number galvanized the musical, helped solve several other focus problems as well, and put everything into perspective.

What you're trying to write simply isn't good enough by your own standards, and your internal barometer is urging you to start again. The above is pretty self-explanatory, but I still can't resist telling a story on myself.

It was 1995, I was writing music and lyrics for the Theatreworks/USA *The Phantom of the Opera,* my first full score using music software and sequencing toys, a liberating, career-changing process for me, and after blasting out four or five songs, great guns, one after the other, *wham, wham, wham . . .*

I hit a snag.

The number I was working on stopped dead in its tracks after the first chorus and refused to budge an inch forward.

I examined the number for all the trouble clues I've just described.

Thematic correctness: check.

Proper character motivation: check.

Credibility in context: check.

Yet for four days I procrastinated before starting work, and when I did start, quickly became very tired—a sure sign for me that something's hinky.

Day four it occurred to me. I pressed the playback button, listened to that first chorus I'd composed . . . and I suddenly sat up straighter and said, out loud, to no one in particular:

"I know why this is so hard to write. Because it *sucks!*"

Everything about the song was correct except the actual execution. I simply wasn't doing my best work; after a fashion I'd been phoning it in: musically it was relying on stale tricks of mine and lyrically it was facile but lazy. I finally embraced the notion that I had to start the song again from scratch, using the same dramatic premise and objective—but just being harder on myself. And that simple decision turned the tide.

FEAR ITSELF

There is one more symptom of the mythical writer's block, and I offer it in all seriousness: It's *thinking* that you have writer's block.

Never let that demon possess you. Go over your checklist of possible problems. Use your collaborator as a sounding board. You may *need* to write an initial false draft as a means of discovering the later, true one, but by the same token, don't *force* writing that feels unnatural. Step back, analyze, regroup, reapproach.

Father Merrin couldn't provide you with a more powerful exorcism. . . .

8
CHAPTER

It Ain't Kid Stuff
or:
Writing Musicals for Young Audiences

TRUTH

HERE'S HOW YOU WRITE MUSICAL THEATRE FOR CHILDREN:

You don't.

You write for yourself.

All right, you caught me, that's not exactly so—when looked at from a certain angle, there are non-adult considerations, and some Theatre for Young Audience (commonly called TYA) musicals are designed to not only satisfy them, but meet them head on. These shows strive to reach the kids via understanding of their vocabularies, their interests, their "target age" level of maturity—and the (sometimes token) educational mandate.

And there's also a level of appropriateness to be maintained: In most TYA marketplaces—and under the ægis of most TYA producers—language and subject matter dare not be provocative in the wrong way; you can't invoke profanity, sexuality, or, assuming a secular context, religious iconography.

From another angle though, the dictum that you don't write for children but for yourself is the absolute truth. Because you have to believe in what you write: you have to embrace the sensibility, better yet embody it. Because—as with any other kind of writing—if you're doing your job inauthentically, or worse, patronizingly, the audience will resist you. And oh, do you ever not want to face the wholesale resistance of children.

As with any mainstream project, you have to make doing it right, honoring the craft, your first priority. Don't try to second-guess audience taste or "commercialize" the project—that's a fool's game.

Your mission is to imbue kids with the wonder of theatre. And to keep your own wonder alive in the process.

After that it's about money.

ART AND COMMERCE

Before you do anything, get a grip on what you're trying to accomplish, and why. There are many outlets for TYA material, but few support the development process of A-level musical theatre (or pay much attention to its needs, or principles of craft), and fewer still provide financial remuneration worth consideration. And those few are the organizations you need to target. (You may find the "Children's Theatre Resource Webpage," at http://faculty-web.at.northwestern.edu/theater/tya, to be helpful in this regard.)

Playwright Robert Anderson famously said, "You can make a killing in the theatre, but not a living." In the arena of TYA theatre, however, the reverse is truer: given a moderate personal overhead, a steadily produced writer can make a living from royalties but not a killing. (Actually, this depends upon how big a piece you have of a given show [a composer-lyricist makes more than a lyricist or a composer], how long your shows run, and so on. You can at least significantly relieve some financial stress and buy yourself more time to write your "regular" musicals, keeping your creative muscles in fighting trim all the while.)

So unless you're driven beyond pragmatism, don't waste your time inventing original TYA musicals that you'd hope to "place" with a viable—meaning financially worthwhile—TYA production outfit. First of all, the viable marketplace for them is just about nonexistent. Second of all, no offense intended, the viable marketplace that *does* exist isn't much interested in your self-generated kid shows. The TYA musical marketplace is about high-profile salability: properties that can be easily pitched to the buyers, who are primarily schools, supplemented here and there by community groups, regional theatres, and organizations that book family theatre events.

This salability breaks down into three categories:

1. **"Brand-name" titles.** These can be mainstream classics or recognizable children's books—the latter of which can run from popular YA novels (*Harriet the Spy*), to expanded fairy tales (*Goldilocks and the Three Bears*), to trademarked franchises for which the production company options the rights (*Where's Waldo?*, *Babar*, *Curious George*, *Reading Rainbow*). My own shows for Theatreworks/USA were *The Phantom of the Opera* and *Les Misérables* (which was fondly referred to as *Les Miz Babies* and *Junior Miz*). The titles were suggested to me by Theatreworks in both cases. I'd never have had—as William Goldman's *Soldier in the Rain* would have put it—the aw-dassity to suggest them myself. But I was happy to take the money for doing them.
2. **Historical figures** (*Young Abraham Lincoln, Paul Robeson*) **and events** (*Freedom Train*, about how black slaves escaped from the South to the North during the Civil War years).
3. **Issues relevant to the school-age experience,** such as illiteracy (*Class Clown*) and divorce (*When the Cookie Crumbles . . .*). These make up the *very* few original musicals (that is, not based on preexisting source material), and they are often—though not always—notoriously low sellers. But TYA outfits keep cautiously gambling with them, because they fill an important niche and occasionally one will hit.

Note too that in any category there may be a mandate to target a specific age group. *The Three Little Pigs* is obviously for the youngest, *Phantom* was aimed at the oldest. Paradoxically, when a show visits a school, teachers of all age groups want to get their kids in on the event, no matter the recommendation on the promo material, so *any* show is a test of how well you can entertain *anybody*. And it's continually astonishing to observe just how much sophistication a young group can take, and just how much silliness an older group is willing to tolerate. So long as it's clear and well done and doesn't patronize, a TYA show can survive the gamut handily.

GETTING THE GIG

While TYA outfits typically—though not exclusively—look to newer and/or younger writers, they won't go near you unless they know and like your work. So have your samples of previous work ready, demos, lyric sheets, scripts, etc. If a representative of the organization can see your work in performance, so much the better. (You don't need an agent to make initial contact with a TYA group—but having one doesn't hurt. More on agents in a bit.)

Okay. Let's say you've jumped the initial hurdles. You're a candidate for the game. Now they're receptive to you.

Commissions come about in two ways:

1. **The producing organization asks you to work on a specific project.** They have a title, or an idea, and they bring it to you— usually with the notion that your imprimatur will be a good match for the material. (When Jay Harnick called me about *Phantom of the Opera,* he announced " . . . and you're the only one who can do it!" Of course this was humorous hyperbole, but he also knew I liked thrillers, and he was especially fond of my "ten-minute" musical mystery *Pulp*—so there was some pragmatic reasoning behind the quip.)

2. *You* **pitch a project to** *them* to which they respond favorably. This involves understanding what they're into, the limit of their production values, and what their shows are like aesthetically. Thus, it helps to see as many as you can and get an idea of both the range of offerings and those subtle and not-so-subtle things common to each.

For example, aside from the above-mentioned *types* of shows, nearly every Theatreworks/USA show has at least a *patina* of educational value. Thus *Phantom of the Opera* became a parable about how society treats people who are "different"; *Les Misérables* one about how the choices we make have consequences that can ripple out and affect other lives.

Furthermore, you have to contend with a cast no larger than six—the seventh person is the stage manager who runs and maintains the show—plus a modular set that, with the costumes, cast, and sound system, can fit into two minivans. (ArtsPower, a company based in New Jersey, is even more austere: you're limited to *four* actors and *one* minivan.) And speaking of the sound system: the cast performs to prerecorded instrumental tracks (whose sound and orchestrations have become increasingly sophisticated right along with the electronic music technology that produces them). Final tip: It helps to get a list of all the producing outfit's previous and currently developing shows, so you know what public domain properties to avoid, what franchises they've already optioned, and never have to hear sentences like, "Oh, didn't you know? Oler and Hubbard have *already* done a *Secret Garden* for us!"

And Both Roads Lead Here

Even if the TYA producers respond to you favorably as a potential writer, it's likely that you'll be asked to write *some* songs and/or sample scenes on spec. Doesn't matter that the honchos know and like your work, doesn't matter that their knowing makes spec-work seem a superfluous step; some TYA producers will hedge their bets unless they feel that you can negotiate the TYA terrain effectively. They also want to get an idea of how fast you work—and how much the samples you deliver resemble the product both sides talked about in the abstract.

Even if you don't have to write *songs* on spec, even if you're a veteran who has successfully worked for the organization before, you may well still have to do a *treatment* on spec—this being a one- or two-page description of your take on the material: how you'll approach or adapt it, what the mission statement (in "educational" terms) is.

Sometimes spec-work is just a formality, a tradition of the process you accept on faith, like Tevye accepting God's will. Sometimes it's a realistic precaution, to make sure everyone's on the same wavelength.

Sometimes, however, it can herald a string of ego-abusing tests—and that's where you have to be vigilant about not taking a project too far without a deal in place. As with any kind of theatre, in TYA too, there are notorious examples of writers who fell for the okeydoke of one producer or another wanting to see "just a little more" at every step deeper into the process, writers who paid for their naïveté with their self-esteem, and no production to show for it. At a certain point, the quality of the work is moot, and if you're not being paid, you're not being treated with respect. And it's not likely to change.

That's why it's vital to have a representative watching your back *if possible* once work of any sort begins in earnest, and *certainly* when you get to the contract stage, even if you're told the deal is standard. There are always fine points particular to each show and its authors that are fodder for negotiation, and a "basic" deal is merely a jumping-off point. If you can't get an agent, call Volunteer Lawyers for the Arts—1 East 53rd Street, 6th Floor, New York, NY 10022-4201, (212) 319-2787, www.vlany.org—and at least get an "eagle" to peruse the papers before you sign anything.

But let's say nobility prevails on both sides, and the treatment passes muster. Now the project is green-lit.

PROCESS

That brings you to the development phase.

In this section, I'm using the Theatreworks/USA process—the one I know from experience—as a template. It's probably the most efficient and comprehensive development procedure for TYA fare there is—which would make sense, as TW/USA have been the preeminent producers of TYA theatre in the country for most of their half-century history. But other established companies I've learned about seem to follow a *similar* template, so I daresay it's more or less the norm. (That said, I'd be more than in a little interested in any significant variations you find Out There, for sharing in a future edition of this book.)

The development phase breaks down into three steps. (Each one is worth progressively more advance money, by the way. In business terms, this is what's called a "step deal," the particulars of which will be detailed in your contract. Note too that the advance—paid against royalties—is small, about half what you'd make on an off-Broadway contract, as arguably befits a show that is half the usual length.)

1. **Round-table reading of the first draft.** Sometimes the producers call for this (they did with the Barron/Spencer *Les Misérables*), sometimes you do it yourself (as Rob Barron and I did—twice—with *Phantom*), but it's a vital step. A group of actors are assembled to do a "cold" (unrehearsed) reading, as a favor or for a really nominal fee; during which the songwriter(s) jump in and play the score as scenes lead to songs—just to get a rough sense of the piece *off* the page. How big a reality check this step turns out to be varies, due to the informality of the event . . . often it's no more than an affirmation that you're headed in the right direction. But if you're *not* headed in the right direction, and your invitees are encouraged to be candid with their reactions, this is a good time—and a great way—to spot the red flags. (You won't get paid for the round-table reading per se, but there is payment for delivery of the completed script which makes a reading possible.)
2. **Two-week workshop.** Just what it says, and it's a workshop like any other . . . the big difference being that the invited audiences

for your scheduled performances (usually two on the same day)
will include kids.

3. **Mini-tour.** This is the equivalent of previews—more accurately,
   the equivalent of the once-common out-of-town tryout. Your
   show will play somewhere between six to ten performances,
   depending upon how well its *title* is "performing" with the
   buyers—*Phantom of the Opera* had a few more test drives than
   usual—in various local and regional venues. Where TW/USA is
   concerned, these whistle stops generally consist of Town Hall in
   Manahttan, Colden Auditorium at Queens College, Hofstra
   University, on Long Island, and a theatre in Red Bank, New
   Jersey, among a few others. In most aspects, the mini-tour
   performances reflect the eventual cross-country tour process: two
   minivans transport cast, production stage manager (PSM), set,
   and costumes; the cast and PSM load the set prior to performance, strike it after, and reload the minivans. What's *unique* to
   the mini-tour is that the authors, director, and producers—in a
   separate car—travel to the performance sites as well. You watch
   the show, clock the audience response, take notes, meet on what
   you've seen, rewrite accordingly. New stuff goes into rehearsal
   as soon as possible for subsequent performances. The mini-tour
   tends to be a four-week process: two weeks of pure rehearsal, two
   weeks of performing and fixing as required.

4. **Cross-country tour.** Generally this is the finished show—your
   contractual obligation to keep writing is usually over—but there
   is a window for volunteering those perfectionist revisions, if you
   believe they're needed, before the tour begins and between
   semesters when the tour shuts down. (During the *Les Misérables*
   mini-tour I was never able to solve the musical sequence between Jean Valjean and the Monsignor who gives him the
   candlesticks . . . I had simply run out of brain cells. But I replen-
   ished them during the downtime after, cracked the problem, and
   the unexpected new material debuted—to TW/USA's pleasant
   surprise—at the first reading by the new cast for the fall tour.)

PLAYERS

As much as possible, you must actor-proof your material during the
above steps. Because the octane and maturity of available performers
diminishes with each step. And with good reason.

Experienced, established, mature-minded actors will happily try to accommodate a two-week workshop in town to their schedules, if there's a pleasant prior relationship in place—or if the project and/or creative team are intriguing enough.

The pool of A-listers gets smaller with the mini-tour. Start including the chores of scenery-schlepping, loading and striking, rising at 6:00 or 7:00 a.m. to meet the van and be ready for a 10:00 a.m. performance, and the gig becomes somewhat less attractive. But at least it's still in town and the commitment is usually no more than a month. So very respectable talents, whose careers haven't yet put them "above" all that, are still game.

The cross-country tour is a whole different enchilada. The pay sucks, and the road-warrior stuff is a continual test of personal and professional stamina. You have to compromise, sometimes mightily, for the best available people willing to endure the rigors. You can luck out, of course: a great young talent needing her Equity card is a good prospect; so is that rare performer who enjoys the TYA tour life and likes the casting odds that come with being a corporate favorite team player; so is the seasoned pro with a rein on his ego who needs work during a dry spell. But you're equally or more likely to have to settle for an unvarnished new college grad right out of the boonies whose biggest assets are the right physical type, a decently convincing persona, an *acceptable* voice, and enthusiasm.

WIGGLES AND THE BAD BUZZ

In general, you work on a TYA show as you'd work on a mainstream show . . . with the same care, tradecraft and attention to detail. But you learn to develop a heightened sense of showmanship. For there is a sense in which TYA shows must never come to a rest. Not and get caught at it anyway.

The most startling difference between performing for kids and performing for adults is that there is no room for misinterpretation—a TYA crowd expresses both pleasure and boredom in unsubtle terms. If they're with you, they're either silent, laughing, applauding, cheering or—in the case of some rougher inner-city groups—abuzz with chat about what's happening onstage. (It's a different sound than the buzz of restlessness or apathy; it takes a few trials by fire to distinguish the contrast, and it can be unnerving the first time you live—or die—through it.)

Conversely, if the kids are *not* with you, they start to fidget and chatter *instantly*. For the workshop of *Phantom* I had a song called "One Fateful Night," in which the Phantom describes the events that disfigured him and led him to take on his mysterious identity. An eerie aria with a slow build, a real performer's turn that Sheldon Harnick had called "a power-house," it told a riveting story. Or would have, if the kids had cared a rat's rear end for it. Their attention dropped out—I'm not exaggerating—at the intro music *before the first syllable*. It wasn't going to be a kid-friendly song and the audience *smelled it coming*. Barbara Pasternak, who now heads TW/USA, calls these danger spots "wiggle moments."

The good news is, when you find the alternate solution that *does* work for kids, you have, invariably and in spite of yourself, made the show better *as a show on its own terms*, quite apart from the kids' reaction. It's a fascinating phenomenon.

KIDS RULE—AND KID RULES

What follows are the TYA-specific principles that can help you avoid several time and work-consuming traps in advance. And the *bad* buzz they lead to.

1. **Overt romance is the enemy**—yukky stuff that kids find embar-
    rassing or fodder for ridicule—unless it's played *very* lightly or
    for laughs. *Sarah, Plain and Tall* managed an uncharacteristic
    coup, because the romance between the adults was always
    presented from the perspective of the observing children, a
    brother and sister whose mom had died; and when it culminated
    in a kiss at the *very* end, as funny as it was sweet, it symbolized a
    broken family being made once again whole, the widower farmer
    dad and the new stepmom "consummating" their attraction in
    an unusual TYA confluence of thematic and story elements. By
    contrast, the Spencer-Barron *Phantom* illustrates the far more
    representative approach: There is definitely *some* emotional
    chemistry between our Christine and Erik (Phantom), *but it dare
    not speak its name*. The romance is *implicit*, and emerges out of the
    nonromantic ways in which they express concern for, help—and
    at times battle with—each other.
2. **Lecturing is out.** Anything that smacks of overt lesson teaching
    ("Do you know what the sections of an orchestra are, boys and

girls? Well . . . ") is death. Kids see through the lame camouflage of "entertainment" and tune out faster than you can say *Sunrise Semester*. Also lethal is any scene in which one character *righteously berates or punishes another* for misbehavior, bad manners, or other wrongdoing. It's one thing if—as in *Les Misérables*—the bad guy (Javert) *maltreats* the good guy (Valjean) by way of *unjust* discipline, because that's conflict, and kids root for an underdog with whom they identify. But the moment you evoke a chastising authority figure—which is precisely where I got into trouble with the *Les Miz* candlestick scene cited earlier—you're playing to a wall of chattering rejection. Kids don't want to know from finger-wagging; they get enough of that in real life.

3. **Ballads are minefields.** You can successfully present one, but not until the story and characters are well established— and even then, *something needs to be happening* in the song. At the very least, the song needs to dramatize an effort to *make* something happen. Which leads to the final rule:

4. **The in-one solo number will not hold stage.** Doesn't mean you can't write a number for solo character, nor that you can't exploit an opportunity to have a character sing private thoughts . . . but the classic convention of *song as dramatic aside*, unaccompanied by activity, will not find a home in your TYA arsenal. You don't want to be frenetic or impose activity for its own sake—but kids will absolutely refuse to sit still for a character simply planting his feet and singing. Solos have to be designed to absorb or enhance action. Ideally, this action is organic and reflects the objective of the character . . . but stage business and choreography are of enormous help—as are the presence of other characters and/or having story progress marked by scene interludes between verses. Unlike the other kid rules, which hearken directly to levels of young audience maturity and social development, this "no in-one solo" rule is more of an enigma. Since kids will sit still for balladeers like Raffi, I've never heard the "why" of it explained satisfactorily. But it is an immutable truth.

POLITICS, OR: THINKING WITHIN THE BOX

Most long-established TYA producers are conservative. They may experiment with artistic approaches *occasionally*, but the budgets are restricted, creative philosophies adjust to the times at a very gradual pace, management may want to keep you on a short leash for what they deem quality control, and the development process hews to tried and true formulæ. None of this is intended as criticism. When an organization has done business successfully, its corporate mentality is what protects them and keeps them generating product that is at least reliable. So you have to maneuver within the system, especially if you hope to write more than one TYA show for the outfit. If you can be partnered with a collaborator or director who has worked successfully for the company before and knows the terrain, so much the better.

But if you enter the TYA world "unescorted," you can nonetheless hold to the following axiom: Wherever possible, your best strategy in a challenging situation is one that draws the least attention to itself as a strategy, or even a response. For if you can make your secret triumph *seem* like a win-win situation . . . it probably is.

Two examples:

1. One writer I know arranges for late deadlines and rarely turns in his work early. And he well could; he's talented and fast. But he also knows that the less time his producers have to scrutinize the material before rehearsals, the less they'll start second-guessing his intentions. Their reactions are limited to a gut response the writer finds useful, and interference is kept to what he considers a manageable level. Moral: know when time is on your side.

2. A workshopping composer, not being a pianist, did her daily revisions via software sequencing and synths. Her TYA producers balked at the unusual process; for to maintain a master show-reel, her digital tracks had to be nightly tranferred to old-fashioned spliceable tape at a private studio, and the cost was mounting. Rather than let the situation become a stalemate, she thought creatively . . . and realized that her producers' TYA tours had begun using lightweight DAT and CD players—replacing a number of hernia-weight reel-to-reel "portables" that were now collecting dust in an electronics storage room. Pro machines, these retired units not only played, but also *recorded*—so she simply asked the producers to let her have one. Thereafter, she made all reel transfers *herself*—protecting her work method while *eliminating* studio costs altogether. Moral: understand and use the available resources.

EDUCATIONAL VALUE

Aside from the advantages cited above, writing TYA musicals provides one more perk—one I never expected, but that I cherish each day:

It makes you better at doing the grown-up stuff.

The heightened showmanship you develop to keep children entertained enhances your ability to please adults. The TYA experience makes you forever mindful of stage pictures, of avoiding waste, of not testing audience patience. Though an adult effort allows you access to a more involved, mature vocabulary, it's truly no more sophisticated an endeavor where *the work* is concerned.

You get better at reading, *feeling* an *adult* audience. At clocking the wiggle moments they're too polite to chatter through. At recognizing the point when interest drops, when the tension leaves the auditorium.

Truth be told, when the grown-ups are sending you a mixed signal, you can find yourself really missing those unequivocal kids. . . .

9
CHAPTER

Speed Kills, Shift Happens, and Other Homilies
or:
Writing Comedy

I DON'T HONESTLY THINK OF MYSELF AS BEING ANYWHERE near the same comedy level as a number of my colleagues whose prowess would make me terribly jealous if I weren't enjoying myself so much . . . but I somehow manage to get the laughs when I *have* to and because I think it's possible to *eventually* achieve comedy through sheer grunt work (so long as you have talent, a good ear, and a sense of humor), I pass this advice on to those who also have to push their own personal envelopes to find their "funny."

There are five things to keep in mind, if you don't *naturally* fall into writing comedy:

If it feels labored in the writing, you're already in trouble. You'll know you're in the zone when you don't feel the effort of *trying* to be funny. Ironically, this does *not* mean you stop writing the crappy song; sometimes the pre-doomed composition is the preparation, the lab experiment that leads to the *right* song. It can help shape your thinking, guide you toward asking the right questions of yourself, eliminate the wrong approach, and define the problem to be solved more accurately.

An altered perspective can be your lifeline. Rather than looking at a subject head-on, shift the frame of reference. Take "It's a Fish" by Sheldon Harnick (music by Jerry Bock), from *The Apple Tree*. An evening of three one-act musicals—tenuously connected by each being a variation on the man-woman-devil triangle—its first act is based on Mark Twain's *The Diary of Adam and Eve*. At this point in the story, Eve has just given birth to their first son. Neither Adam nor Eve understands the concept of a baby; until now the world has existed of only them and the animals. Her lullaby, "Go to Sleep, Whatever You Are" alternates with the stanzas of "It's a Fish" from Adam. (As a sidebar, note how the song also develops Adam's innocence and neatly depicts the passage of time, obviating the need for any narrative explication. Note too how the punch line smartly assumes our knowledge of the Adam and Eve legend, without spelling out an obvious detail, making us complicit in the joke.)

ADAM

I just got back from a hunting trip up north and found that Eve had caught some new kind of animal.

NOW I COULD SWEAR
THAT IT'S A FISH,
THOUGH IT RESEMBLES US IN EV'RY WAY BUT SIZE.
SHE GIVES IT MILK,
AND EV'RY NIGHT,
SHE PICKS IT UP AND PATS AND PETS IT WHEN IT
    CRIES.
I ALWAYS KNEW EVE PITIED FISH,
BUT IT'S RIDICULOUS TO MAKE THEM HOUSEHOLD
    PETS.
SHE SAYS IT'S NOT A FISH.
I SAY IT IS A FISH . . .
'CAUSE IT SURROUNDS ITSELF WITH WATER
ALMOST EV'RY CHANCE IT GETS!

IT'S NOT A FISH.
FISH NEVER SCREAM.
BUT THIS ONE DOES, THOUGH ON OCCASION IT
    SAYS, "GOO."
ITS LEGS ARE LONG.
ITS ARMS ARE SHORT.
SO I SUSPECT THAT IT'S A KIND OF KANGAROO.
AND SINCE IT CAME,
I PITY EVE.
SHE'S GOTTEN MADDER BY THE MINUTE AND IT
    SHOWS.

JUST NOW I SAID TO HER
THAT I WOULD MUCH PREFER
TO HAVE IT STUFFED FOR MY COLLECTION
AND SHE PUNCHED ME IN THE NOSE!

IT'S GROWING TEETH!
AND IT CAN BITE!
AND I'M CONVINCED THAT WHAT WE HAVE HERE
    IS A BEAR!
I'M WORRIED SICK!
AND EVE IS NOT!
SHE BURNED THE MUZZLE THAT I MADE FOR IT TO
    WEAR!
I'VE SEARCHED THE WOODS,
I'VE BAITED TRAPS,
AND YET I COULDN'T FIND ITS SISTER OR ITS
    BROTHER.
AND WHILE I'VE HUNTED FAR AND WIDE,
WHILE EVE HAS HARDLY STEPPED OUTSIDE . . .
I'LL BE *DAMNED* IF SHE DIDN'T CATCH ANOTHER!

Keep it real and take refuge in character. This is *especially* true for those who don't have an automatic comedy reflex. If you don't think *jokes*, think *psychology*. Combine the idiosyncrasies of the character with what he/she wants; generally—if the resultant behavior is honest within the parameters defined by the story and its milieu—that will produce laughter, because even in the extreme, the character will be recognizably human.

For example: here are the first two stanzas from "Need to Know," a lyric I wrote for the one-act science fiction musical *Her Pilgrim Soul*, the second half of *Weird Romance*. Daniel, a young research scientist, is trying to motivate his bewilderingly reluctant colleague and boss into further investigating a techno-mystery. Daniel does this by tracing the development of his own passion:

I'M TEN YEARS OLD, I'M AT THE LOCAL DUPLEX:
THE SCIENCE FICTION MATINEE AT TWO.
I DON'T RECALL THE MOVIE, BUT THE ALIENS
    WERE GROOVY

AND I WONDERED, "HOW'D THEY MAKE THE
    ACTORS BLUE?"
SO—WHEN I GET HOME I FILL THE TUB WITH
    FIZZIES . . .
THIRTY-FORTY FIZZIES, PURPLE GRAPE.
I SOAK FOR SEVEN HOURS. I GET THESE FUNNY
    STREAKS.
THEY WON'T COME OFF IN SHOWERS,
PEOPLE LAUGH AT ME FOR WEEKS.
BUT I KNEW.
THOUGHT I KNEW.
AND AT TEN THAT WAS A MIGHTY HEADY BREW.
ON MY SKIN,
IN MY HAIR . . .
AND I FELL IN LOVE WITH RESEARCH THEN AND
    THERE.
AND I THOUGHT,
"CHECK IT OUT:
I'VE LOCKED INTO WHAT MY LIFE IS ALL ABOUT."
AND THUS IT DIDN'T MATTER WHEN THEY
    CHUCKLED AT MY HUE.
I WAS TEN.
I WAS BLUE.
AND I KNEW.

IN JUNIOR HIGH I'M TAKIN' HEALTH AND HYGIENE.
BIRTH CONTROL TECHNIQUES ARE WHERE WE'RE
    AT.
THE TEACHER'S GOIN' ON HOW BEST AND STRON-
    GEST IS THE CONDOM,
AND I'M WONDERING, "WELL, JUST HOW STRONG
    IS THAT?"
SO—COMES THE YEARLY SCIENCE COMPETITION . . .
I SNAP THE SHEET, MY PROJECT IS UNVEILED:
"THE RUBBER PROPHYLACTIC—HOW IT FUNCTIONS
    UNDER STRESS."
THE FACES ON THE FACULTY, YOU'D THINK I WORE
    A DRESS.
BUT I KNEW.

HAD IT GRAPHED.
FOR THE RUBBER GRIP, THE RESERVOIR, THE SHAFT.
HAD MACHINES TESTING LENGTH,
LIQUID MERCURY FOR GAUGING TENSILE
    STRENGTH.
HOW'D I DO?
HARD TO TELL.
SEE, THE GIRLS THOUGHT IT WAS INT'RESTING AS
    HELL.
THOUGH THE GUYS WERE DOUBLED OVER,
AND THE PRINCIPAL, HOO-HOO:
HE'S OFFENDED,
I'M SUSPENDED.
BUT I KNEW.

Believe it or not, there was not one consciously written joke in it. But I defaulted to Daniel's colorfully colloquial demeanor, his insatiable curiosity, his natural obsession with detail and his quick perception. That created the short-phrase energy bursts and pulse of his passion . . . and led inevitably to the line, "But I knew." It struck just the right attitude to conclude each phase of the argument. But like Ethel Merman, he also had rhythm. And that leads me to the fourth point:

Comedy is (usually) fast. At least the phrase intended to release laughter is. It has to come at the listener like something out of a staple gun, and most of the time the punch line is really a sucker punch. Which is to say, you head toward someplace that will (in retrospect) be inevitable; but that upon arrival is a total surprise . . . either because the audience's expectations have been reversed or because the setup has been so skillfully realized that *where you were headed was a mystery that the punch line resolved.* That said: **Comedy can be (on rare occasion)** *deliberately* **slow,** achieving its laughter by subversive repetition or variation of the expected ("The Internet Is for Porn" from *Avenue Q* by Lopez and Marx)— slowing sometimes to *such* a crawl that the *suspension* of resolution is what's funny ("The Grass Is Always Greener" from *Woman of the Year* by Kander and Ebb). The set-up can be as long or as short as context dictates. But the punchline has to be a Ninja hit.

Of the numerous gratifying laughs my comedy lyrics have gotten, the following one produces, arguably, the biggest. It's in a song called "Art and Commerce" from *The Apprenticeship of Duddy Kravitz.* The story takes place in Montreal, circa 1950. Duddy Kravitz, a hustling Jewish kid from the St. Urbain Street ghetto, is trying to raise money to buy lakefront property, and he decides the best business venture for the capitalization is producing private films of bar mitzvahs and weddings. At a night class, he meets a washed-up, British, bibulous, alcoholic film director named Peter John Friar. Duddy takes Friar out for a drink, to try and interest him in the deal on a commercial level. Friar, however, wants to be stroked as an artiste; additionally, Friar's so drunk that he keeps confusing Duddy's name with that of another young movie mogul.

FRIAR

BUT I WARN YOU, THALBERG—

DUDDY

KRAVITZ.

FRIAR

THERE'S JUST ONE DIRECTOR HERE, THALBERG—

DUDDY

KRAVITZ.

FRIAR

SO NO INTERFERENCE HERE, THALBERG.

DUDDY

KRAV—

FRIAR

I EXPECT A FREE HAND, AND NO MISTAKE.
MIND STILL MEETING THERE, THALBERG?

DUDDY

KRAVITZ. SO FAR.

FRIAR

LET'S TALK MOVIES THEN, THALBERG.

DUDDY

KRAVITZ. WE ARE.

FRIAR

I'LL DESCRIBE—WHAT'S YOUR NAME AGAIN?

DUDDY
THALBERG. NO, JESUS—

FRIAR
DESCRIBE FOR YOU, JESUS, THE FILM I SHALL MAKE!

Again, I didn't consciously write a joke. What I did was mildly exaggerate a facet of Friar's behavior, which is his dottiness when drunk. And I exploited the use of music, which encourages repetition. The misnomer *Thalberg*, and Duddy's correction of it, start to become a mantra, and a lulling one, so that when Friar achieves just enough clarity to suspect he's getting the name wrong, it is *Duddy* who becomes momentarily absentminded, and falls right into the refrain. But because he's stone sober, he jolts out of his mistake with an exclamation—as most of us would—but the exclamation is a proper name. Which becomes Friar's answer and in turn obliterates Duddy's chance to set the record straight. That name being *Jesus* leads to the fifth and final point:

The power of irreverence—when appropriate (which is nearly always)—can never be underestimated. Any time you think you've earned the right to—

- shatter a sacred cow;
- revel in subversion;
- do/say the thing that everyone thinks but no one dares articulate; or
- deliver an organically derived moment of shock value—

—you must at least try it. Comedy is often at its best when it's dangerous. Not mean-spirited—there's a fine line between gleeful naughtiness (Richard Pryor) and the wrong kind of nastiness (Andrew Dice Clay)—but you can always experiment with tone and proportion until you find the balance.

In fact, that may be the single one-size-fits-all truth about comedy: The trick is getting the right combination of tone, proportion, and balance.

Well, tone, proportion, balance, and timing.

No, wait: tone, proportion, balance, timing, and instinct.

Right. I think. (Tone, pro*por*tion, balance, timing, per*spec*—) Aw, *hell*.

Okay—this is it, this is it, stay with me, I got it now . . . .

10
CHAPTER

Well, Maybe Thou Shalt Steal
or:
Influences

I HAVE OCCASIONALLY ENCOUNTERED NEW MUSICAL WRITERS who shy away from listening to other musicals for fear of being unduly influenced. This is so flabbergasting to me I barely know how to respond. One of the most effective learning tools is structural and stylistic imitation (of many sources, not just musical theatre). I mean, presumably one enters an artistic field because one has been moved by artists and works *within* that field—*why shut down the very signal that got you jazzed in the first place?* And once you're a grounded pro, finding the influences that can inform the texture of a given show or score often leads to exhilarating inspiration toward something new and original.

Ironically, where the subject of *my* "influences" is concerned, I find that for all my analytical powers, my obsession with construction and deconstruction, I am *almost purely* a creature of instinct.

I do believe this much, however: one way or the other, our styles are an amalgam of the styles that hit us during our formative years. And I believe that what creates a writer's style is the way that individual chooses—consciously or unconsciously—to combine those "chemicals."

Like most theatre composers of the newer breed, I occasionally betray the unavoidable Sondheim influence; but sometimes even more pervasive are the echoes of Lalo Schifrin, Earle Hagen, John Barry, Michel Legrand, Burt Bacharach, Elmer Bernstein, Hugo Montenegro, Henry Mancini, even, God help me, Vic Mizzy—the film composers who warped my brain growing up—and (I was recently surprised to realize) there's also a healthy, sublimated dose of Harvey Schmidt. Add theatre orchestrators Eddie Sauter and Jonathan Tunick to season the stew.

As a wordsmith, I've had people point out the chattiness, aggressiveness, and unabashed colloquialism of my style—and sure enough, the writers who most struck me early on were signature stylists of popular fiction: Evan (Ed McBain) Hunter, Walter Wager, the Goldman brothers (William and James), Warren Murphy, Richard ben Sapir, Harlan Ellison, Theodore Sturgeon, Stephen King, Richard Matheson, Rod Serling, Charles Beaumont, even career pulpsmiths like take-no-prisoners rightwinger Lou Cameron, hardcore poet Jim Thompson, the high kitsch one-and-only Mike Avallone—and playwright Herb Gardner found his way in there, too.

All these distinctive voices and more intermingle with my life experience to create the composite voice that is mine; yet I find it terribly difficult to assimilate *new* influences today the way I used to back then, as the formative years are over and the earmarks of my writer's persona have long since been established. Not that I don't admire, and expose myself to, new and contemporary voices all the time; I'd be mad (and self-destructive) if I didn't. They just don't take root permanently at a primal level. It's as if that space on the personal hard drive is used up.

But a writer has to keep maturing, or he stagnates and dies, creatively. He can't keep going back to the same well all the time.

So I find that the trick is to pick up new *filters*. Like coffee filters, they're disposable, *temporary* influences, thus they don't have a profound lasting effect; but they're the things I strain my style *through* on a per-case basis, that inform the differences between each project, that allow me to change and update my vocabulary, to continue experimenting, even as my author's identity remains a constant. Unlike my primary influences, which were absorbed on an unconscious level, these are deliberately "recruited": I collect them as I need them.

Sometimes it involves combining obvious research with personal taste and what feels right. For example:

- Obvious research: while I was writing the young audience *Les Misérables* score for Theatreworks/USA, I had a few albums' worth of French music on hand for quick inspiration and "brain-freshening."
- Personal taste: All the albums featured twentieth-century music—Françaix, Ravel, Poulenc—well out of the story's

period, but to me they *said* France in a dramatic context better than less anachronistic fare.

- What feels right: except for two numbers, the French music informed the score only in flashes, fills, signature riffs, the use of evocative orchestral patches (like accordion), that kept the nationality present without making it the point of the score.

Sometimes I don't even know an influence is needed right away. When I was commissioned to do the English adaptation of *La Bohème* for the Public Theatre, I was astonished at the original Italian libretto's logical inconsistencies (which I fixed), and challenged by characterizations that I knew would be tough to take in the colloquial English that had earned me the gig in the first place: characterizations I'd have to change on a subtle, internal level, that would not give any *outward* appearance of having been totally reinvented. The opera's four artists—Rodolfo, Marcel(lo), Colline, and Schaunard—were especially off-putting, because they behaved like dilettantes, with a lot of "Oh, the mood is not with me" posturing. I wanted them to be taken seriously as struggling artists, which meant *they* had to take their art—and their obsessive devotion to it—seriously as well. But how, then, to justify their capering, slacking off, and hijinks? I swiveled my office chair and spotted on my bookshelf a volume devoted to the TV series *M*A*S*H*—and as quickly as you could say, "incoming!" I had my answer. Those bohemian boys don't clown around because they're spoiled and effete, I realized; in my version, they'd clown around *to blow off steam, to vent the pent-up anger of constant rejection and relentless poverty.* Just like the doctors at the 4077th, after too many hours of meatball surgery. It made the humor edgier, gave the male bonding the genuine locker-room vitality that had been missing. No one ever knew it, but those scenes with the guys in the loft were my homage to Hawkeye, Trapper, and B.J. in the Swamp.

Sometimes I'm not quite sure what filter I'm looking for; I only know what it's supposed to do for me when I find it. I call these filters "problem solvers," because they address challenges in the material related to *abstract concept* rather than literal connection. They appear as visceral answers to an intellectual riddle. To wit—this from Stephen Sondheim about his score for *Pacific Overtures:*

Japanese music is not tonally like ours at all. There aren't the same frequencies in the notes and they're not hit dead on. That's what makes them sound so twangy. The instruments are not well tempered the way they are in Western music cultures; and they have approximate pitches, so you can't blend them gracefully in any way, shape or form with Western orchestras or with Western voices.

I was searching for a Western equivalent, and one day I hit upon the correlation between the Japanese scale and the music of Manuel de Falla, a [Spanish] composer whose work I admire a lot. [And who also, Sondheim pointed out in an earlier television interview, wrote music that, like Japanese music, would stick with a single tonality for a long time, with little chromatic variance.] So I just started to imitate him. I took the pentatonic scale and bunched the chords together until they resembled that terrific guitar sound. And I was able to relate to it because suddenly it had a Spanish Western feeling and at the same time an Eastern feeling. It seldom occurs to me to write in minor keys, but because I had to have the feeling of Japanese tonality this afforded me the opportunity to do it.

Sometimes the filter is my very motivation for writing in the first place. The following words are those of bestselling novelist Dean Koontz; but almost two decades after my having read them, they still have the power to make *me* consider the choices *I* make as a musical dramatist. He's talking about the process of writing his 1977 novel *The Vision:*

I was interested in *The Vision* primarily because it offered me a chance to engage in a stylistic experiment. One day, looking over a shelf of books in search of something to read, I was suddenly struck with the realization that most horror novels are written in a dense or even baroque style. Oh, certainly *Rosemary's Baby, The Exorcist* and a few others are not baroque, but the majority are. Even Stephen King's books—especially *'Salem's Lot, The Shining* and *The Stand*—have a sort of *modern* baroque quality. I began to wonder what a horror novel would read like if it were written in brisk, stripped-down prose. That made me think of James M. Cain and Dashiell Hammett, and Hammett's name really started my idea pump working at top speed. Could a horror novel be written in a style approximating Hammett's? Could it be told in lean, almost cold prose and still be scary? Could the hard-boiled, tough tone of 1930s detective fiction be adapted to the horror genre with any degree of success? I quickly sat down at my typewriter to give it a try, and *The Vision* turned out to be one of the most exhilarating writing experiences I had had up till that time.

I never, ever know in advance what influence will enhance a given project, what free-associative connection will create the most cathartic and inspired creative causality. So I try to keep my mind open to noncategorical thinking.

Some years ago, librettist Stephen Witkin, my collaborator on *The Fabulist*, gave me a couple of ancient-music recordings to evoke the æsthetic of that long-gone universe. I listened. They were all perfectly tasteful, insightfully selected, thoughtfully submitted for consideration—and bewilderingly, frustratingly useless. What they offered sounded to me familiar, generic, and I ho-hummed my way through the selections. A few days later I put the video of *E.T.: The Extraterrestrial* into my VCR—nostalgic for a film I hadn't seen in over ten years—heard the John Williams score and said, "Ah-*hah!*" Within minutes, all my vinyl John Williams albums were stacked on the floor against my record shelf. I hadn't been in need of period authenticity; I'd needed a refreshed sense of orchestral grace, that would also lend itself to fanfare—for I realized that if I could put my irreverent style through that filter, I could create an epic exoticism, quite apart from the clichés of the genre. In the end, the score bore little resemblance to Williams' style—that had merely been a trigger. But it was one that came by accident.

There are no principles here. But if I have anything to impart, it might be my concern that often, in workshops and readings, sometimes even in full productions, I'm exposed to songs, and occasionally libretti, that seem to have little or *no* sense of influence, lacking muscle or personality, lacking even an awareness of the *need* for muscle or personality. And I wonder: who are these writers listening to, reading, allowing into their souls, to shape their understanding and gut-level reflexes about what we do? Anyone of value? *Anyone at all?*

Many years ago, perhaps as many as twenty-five, I sent Steve Sondheim a cassette of music I liked that I thought he'd like, too. At the time, he was in the middle of working on a new score, and in his thank-you letter he wrote: "I'll listen to it as soon as I need to steal something. Which will probably be tomorrow." And I thought, when I read those words: My God, even *he* . . . .

Without influences, we as writers are nothing. Even as we deny it. William Goldman wrote:

I have always been *only* a storyteller. I was twenty-four when I wrote my first novel, *The Temple of Gold*, and when I entered the playing field, all I brought with me was a sense of story and an ear for dialogue. I did not have the stylistic grace of my beloved Irwin Shaw. I had not the interest or dazzle to try experimental stuff like Joyce. I could not describe like Fitzgerald. I did not have the religious torment of Dostoyevsky or the sweep of Tolstoi or the insanity of Cervantes or the genius of Chekhov and if you think who am I, writing these names down, well, these were the guys that moved me.

The value of a good influence used wisely and judiciously can't be underestimated. It's not plagiarism. You're not copying. You're emulating. You're taking out an unofficial loan, and you're going to pay it back with interest, in the coin of your own individual realm.

After the notorious thief Willie Sutton had retired and become a celebrity, he was asked by a journalist why he'd chosen to rob banks. His famous answer, if regarded metaphorically, might well be ours:

"Because that's where the money is . . . "

CHAPTER

Audio with Pictures
or:
The Art of the Reading

DOUGLAS ADAMS' WONDERFUL SCIENCE FICTION PARODY, *The Hitchhiker's Guide to the Galaxy* has seen many forms, but it started as a series of BBC radio plays, with twelve episodes. The first six episodes were reconceived and redone for records, and while I have the original broadcasts too, the revamped LP (now CD) versions are even sharper, more brilliantly written, sound-designed, directed, and engineered—and more winningly acted (mostly by the same cast).

And it's one of my favorite things in the world.

And as I was listening to it again, I was struck by the very *particular* parameters of the experience. How with voices, effects, timing, music, Adams conjures, quite literally, a universe—a huge, wild, and diversely populated one at that—so effectively that when I think back on it, I remember it with pictures, as if I'd *seen* it.

And, having been through a number of successful readings—i.e., they got their projects to the next step—I realized how many audio storytelling techniques I and my colleagues have adapted for our own use. And by extension, how many *you* might—indeed, *should*—adapt for yours.

THE APPROXIMATION/IMAGINATION GAME

There are several kinds of readings: there's the round-table reading—informal, off-the-cuff, whose sole purpose is to give the authors a very rough sense of what they have.

Then there's the more rehearsed reading—which can be closed to all but the creative team only or open to select invitees—again just for "research" to get a more detailed sense of the show on its feet.

These first two can afford to be rough-hewn, as they're strictly for project insiders and friends of the insiders.

When preparing for rehearsal studio and backers' readings though, you not only have to polish your material as best you can—you also have to factor in another level of showmanship. Never forget the importance of working on the audience's imagination . . . and always remember that the reading is only an *approximation* of the actual musical; therefore you must both *compensate* for the limitations of the venue and let the limitations of the venue work *for* you. And, because the "less is more" principle is in full sway, an audio drama enhanced by certain visual images is not a bad paradigm.

Now—what does working on the audience's imagination mean? It means helping them *mentally fill in* the scope of things that aren't present. These things are scenery, costumes, props, staging, fluidity of change (any change, scenic, emotional, whatever)—and something I'll call non-narrative pacing. It also means helping them *tune out* the distractions and intrusions of the environment, such as the configuration of the room and utilitarian stage directions. (Some stage directions can be quite entertaining, used properly; I distinguish those from utilitarian stage directions, which provide flat information.)

What fills the imagination with many *concrete* details is the *suggestion* of a very few *select* details.

Assuming you've cast your reading meticulously, you have a certain degree of ammo from the start: the faces and bodies of the performers. As each character is met, the audience will begin to project the actor's physicality—and voice—into the mind-movie you're aspiring to create.

You don't want to costume anybody—but you will want what an actor wears to convey an essence of his character. A businessman should wear a jacket and tie; if he's drunk, he might loosen the tie. A young, pushy kid might wear sneakers, jeans, and a Nike shirt. A woman planning a dinner party on the Upper East Side might wear something clingy and casually elegant. For a more whimsical character (say, an elf or a witch), you let tone and taste guide you, but still, the illusion of everyday clothing that just *happens* to be a perfect visual shorthand is key. (You can be *economically* inventive—say, a sports cap with antlers for a talking moose—but *only* if the novelty has enough wit to subliminally say: *What did you* expect *at a reading: Florence Klotz?* The audience is in on the joke, then, and without realizing it, they become co-conspirators.)

By the same token, beware rehearsal wear that can *violate* the mood. You may have cast the perfect actress to play a warm, understanding mother—but if she's sporting spiky punk hair and tight leather, you and your director must request that she soften the first and replace the second. (By the way, that's a scenario from real life; I didn't make it up.)

You don't want to use solid props—they literalize the event and dull the imagination reflex. Mild pantomime for anything hand-held—a pen, a phone, a gun—is enough, and stage directions or dialogue will take care of anything bigger. Exceptions? Here's a very specific one from one of the readings of *The Apprenticeship of Duddy Kravitz,* book and lyrics by me, music by Alan Menken, based on the novel by Mordecai Richler: Our title character—a pushy but ambitious and hard-working teenage kid— is having a hard time on his first day as a waiter at a big Catskills-style summer resort. A businessman, Cohen, calls Duddy over to his table, and in song, lets Duddy know there's a reward for snappy service. In time to the music and lyrics, Cohen produces a hundred-dollar bill and rips it in two. He gives one piece to Duddy, holds the other and sings: "Half now. And later, if I'm happy, no reason we should split up a set, capeesh?" In this kind of exchange, there's no point in hamstringing either the mate- rial or the actor's timing with a spoken stage direction like "Cohen rips the bill in half." We gave the actor a rectangular piece of white paper, the size and shape of currency. He ripped it for real, gave away half, kept half. But here's where we stuck to the principle of suggestion: *It was* only *a piece of white paper.* Not (obviously) a real bill. Not play money. In those very few instances when props seem necessary, it's best if they're recog- nizably *stand-ins* for real props. The cheaper your production values seem—perversely—the better.

SCENERY

There is none. But let's divide this consideration into two subtopics. The world of the reading, and the world of the play.

The World of the Reading

This is your physical plane. Depending upon the shape of the room, the depth of the playing area, there are various ways to arrange the placement of the cast, audience, and sight lines. I remember seeing a reading in which the actor's chairs were arranged in rows that articulated a V fanning out toward the back: the lead characters occupied the seats in the front, secondary the middle, ensemble the rear. However, the playing space was unusually deep, and the audience seats (bleachers) unusually raked and high, so this was a creative and wise adaptation. Always exploit what you have.

What you'll have most times, though, is a decent-sized room configured for a limited playing area and audience seating that does *not* rise. It's best to seat your cast in a semicircular or straight-line row, with your leads nearest center. Depending on cast size, have a few communal music stands for general ensemble use, and another three (four max) in front, with accompanying stools optional. The musical director and piano are usually on either side and a tad in front of this configuration. *Which* side and how *far* front depends upon how much eye contact the musical director will need to make with actors during the presentation, and the optimal unobtrusive angle for same. Though you must never violate the audience comfort or sound-balance zone, there's a great deal of subtle leeway. Let the rehearsal process guide you.

An occasionally used alternative configuration is having the actors seated behind two long tables formed as a V. But I find that tables put a distancing *barrier* between your show and the audience, precluding two of your most powerful tools: proximity and movement.

Proximity affects two things: the relationship of the show to the audience and the relationship of the actors to each other. You don't want to be intrusively in the audience's face, but you *do* want to encourage a certain intimacy of atmosphere. As for the actors, now we're in . . .

The World of the Play

Those front-center music stands are the ones the appropriate featured performers will cross to (script in hand) when they have scenes with each other. This allows the important action to come forward, the configuration of bodies to vary, and the appropriate bodies to interact on a human level—thus maintaining the illusion of an observable universe *that is other than the audience's own.* This movement is a de facto form of staging, but it isn't *real* staging, nor does it *look* as rehearsed as it *has* been.

FLUIDITY OF CHANGE

Scenes, moods, and sometimes tones *shift* in a musical, and thanks to modern technology, theatrical transitions are often cinematically seamless. You can put forth the illusion of this fluidity just by being mindful of a few basic philosophies.

First: once the cast is into their final rehearsals, they should be encouraged to *energize* the reading. Not overact or oversell; but rather, keep pace up, remember the importance of engaging the audience, move from scene to song and back without formality, avoid the conservative patina of stately ceremony that can insidiously invade as a result of natural insecurity. Remember, the actors have learned this material *fast,* and some will subconsciously hedge about leaping, Butch-and-Sundance-like, off the cliff, unless you embolden them to have no shame about it. Nor fear of mistakes—those will happen anyway, it's part of the experience. (Music—transitional underscoring, plus very selective *scene* underscoring—can be a vital component of fluidity.)

Second: promote the aforementioned "non-narrative pacing"—the removal of the narrator who *tells* what's happening when you're better off *showing*. Eliminate stage directions that are read aloud wherever you can. Examine your dialogue carefully: frequently the stage direction is already implicit. Sometimes you can even artfully doctor a line of dialogue to *absorb* the function of a stage direction (you can always change it back later). Or the actors can do a quick bit of business that conveys the information much more efficiently.

Another *Duddy Kravitz* moment: in an early scene, Duddy, provoked, mouths off to his father—who, caught off guard, lashes out. The stage direction in the script is "Max slaps Duddy so hard he falls against the counter." That was too long to read. The first edit was: "Max slaps Duddy." Closer—four syllables. But a slap, if you will, is only one.

The solution? Duddy fired his line at Max, Max registered quick anger in his face, cupped his *left* hand and brought the flat of his *right* hard against it—*crack!*—making the *sound* of the slap. *On* the sound, Duddy whipped his head to the side. There was no physical violence, but you sure felt the blow in the audience. Nonviolent physical contact is *selectively* okay, too. There's no reason why characters who would naturally touch each other shouldn't; and if your performers are game, you can also skip goofy-to-read stage directions like "They kiss."

That said, there are times when performed stage directions can work in your favor if they're phrased, timed, and placed correctly. We had a few in *Duddy Kravitz* that consistently got laughs because they informed what the audience knew about the characters. My favorite was one for Peter John Friar, the washed-up, bibulous, alcoholic film director that Duddy engages to make bar mitzvah movies: "Friar weaves onstage looking through a hand-held film camera as Duddy moves to steady him. Friar seems to be aiming at anything." It works because it has attitude.

Finally, there are times when, in the interest of clarity, stage directions—the utilitarian type—are unavoidable, but nonetheless intrusive. How do you take the curse off *that* paradox? Sometimes you just have to grit your teeth through it, trusting the audience is hip enough to dig the necessity. Sometimes—indeed, most times—you can be crafty, and dodge the bullet.

One last *Duddy* example: we're in Duddy's office. His girlfriend Yvette says: "You're hanging everything on this business of yours and you don't even know if anyone wants it yet."

Duddy bluffs: "A lot you know. I've already got a client."

Yvette: "Forgive me—*who?*"

And Duddy, caught, goes: "Uhh—"

Then he turns about, immediately addressing a new playing space— that of our bill-ripping pal Mr. Cohen, the client Duddy will attempt to hustle at the elder's place of business, a scrap-metal yard.

Cohen calls offstage, "Irving! Dammit, how many times I gotta tell you? The copper you don't mix in with the aluminum!"

Okay, now if your ear for timing is attuned, you understand the gag. Duddy goes "Uhh," Cohen says "Irving!" and the transition is that fast—and because we've met Cohen earlier in the play, and know him to be a tough customer, pretty funny. But the gag's rhythm is *completely* flummoxed by the stage direction between beats. The rehearsal script gives a few details about the yard, but even stripped to the near-nubbin— "The scene shifts. In the background a wall of corrugated sheet metal with the legend: Cohen's Scrap-Metal Works"—the verbiage is too much. *Anything* would be too much. What can you do?

You borrow the cinema trick—the one where you hear the next scene's start-dialogue *overlapping* the previous scene's end-visual. That's what *we* did, and it went like this:

YVETTE

You're hanging everything on this business of yours and you don't even know if anyone wants it yet.

DUDDY

A lot you know. I've already got a client.

YVETTE

Forgive me—*who?*

DUDDY

Uhhh—

COHEN

Irving!

STAGE DIRECTION READER

The scene shifts to Cohen's Scrap-Metal Works.

COHEN

Dammit, how many times I gotta tell you? The copper you don't mix in with the aluminum!

In this manner, Cohen's *voice* is what took us to a new locale, the timing of the joke intact. *Right on the heels of that,* the stage direction *defined* the locale. And *hard upon that,* Cohen *continued* with his line. The stage direction became as unobtrusive as a camera cut, and the flow was unimpeded.

This may sound like a small beat and a small victory—and taken alone, it is—but the more small victories over reading limitations that you can uncover, the more you're likely to win the approximation/imagination game.

Remember the example set by Mr. Adams.

If you get the "radio play" *just right* . . . who knows how far you can go?

12
CHAPTER

Acceptable Margins
or:
Proper Playscript Formatting

THE WAY A SCRIPT SUBMISSION PACKAGE LOOKS IS EXACTLY analogous to the way *you* look. No reasonable person would show up at a black-tie affair in cutoff jeans; nor would he show up for a first date in gaudy, mismatched colors and wearing a propeller beanie. Yet the number of people who submit scripts that are just as inappropriately packaged is mind boggling. The way you present a script and accompanying materials (if any) is just as telling as your table manners, and reveals more about your professionalism—in some cases, even about your emotional stability—than you may realize. I'll assume that everybody knows the basic SASE protocol. This chapter concerns itself with what's *inside* the envelope.

Whether submitting to a competition or for professional consideration, the chances are your script will be read first by a screener, or a panel of screeners. These are the folks who determine whether the script gets passed to the higher-ups for more serious consideration. Screeners can be anything from young, self-important flunkies to serious professionals with significant credits. You have no control over that. The only thing you can control is what they see. Sure, occasionally a badly formatted script will get a stamp of approval; but that script has to be good enough to overcome a negative first impression—and will most likely have to overcome that negative first impression again and again, at every step of consideration. Even at its best, it will always advertise the writer's lack of professional experience. Why start out with that handicap? Remember, your objective is to *get your script past the readers*, and *get your project into play*.

THE SYNOPSIS: YOUR SECRET WEAPON

Not all competitions and production offices ask for a synopsis. But even though, ideally, we artists want a reader to "experience the play as written," it's a good idea to include a synopsis anyway. Here's why: a screener will rarely read your entire play—even if she likes it. Especially with competitions, there are so many scripts to peruse (for, generally, so little money per script) that the name of the screener's game is to blast through as many as possible as *quickly* as possible. The synopsis tells the reader how (and often how well) the play is structured, what the play is about, what kind of play it is, and stylistically what it's trying to accomplish. And in providing a quick overview, it gives the reader license to skip around, to read entirely and *carefully* those sections that she finds potentially interesting, rather than paging quickly through less "important" sections and perhaps, carelessly scanning at random. Since the screener will probably only sample your script anyway, make it easy for her to do so *efficiently*.

Often, synopses are clipped to scripts or script covers as a separate page; I think it makes more sense to include it as part of the script proper, right after the title page, so that it never gets lost or misplaced.

Keep the synopsis to a single-spaced single page. There's no law that says you must write it dryly, or solemnly . . . but don't overhype it or get into self-promotion or anything that smacks of ad copy or faux quote ads. This is a Jack Webb just-the-facts-ma'am document. It's there to *help* you; don't abuse the opportunity.

REHEARSAL SCRIPT FORMAT

One of the most common errors made by beginning playwrights and librettists is emulating the style of scripts as published in *books*. That is *not* the same as rehearsal script format. Most play publishers compress plays into a format that is suitable for reading purposes *only*—and *un*suited to practical use—at the very least, inefficient. They do this in order to eliminate white space (thus saving on paper) and to create a print environment for the layman reader that more closely resembles prose.

(Ironically, this also includes theatre publishers like Samuel French and Dramatists Play Service.)

There is only *one* accepted rehearsal script format in the United States. And there's no excuse anymore for scripts that show the earmarks of having been produced at a typewriter. Word-processing programs are the order of the day, just as the sophistication of music hardware and software has invalidated the legitimacy of demos recorded on amateur, rather than professional, equipment. Your script should have a clean, *conservative*, desktop publishing appearance.

Script Covers and Title Pages

Submit scripts bound in a no-frills report cover or binder built to hold 8½ x 11 sheets in three-hole-punch style—plastic bind or velobind style can be acceptable too, but they're unusual enough to give the impression of grandstanding if the presentation is not meticulous. If your binder utilizes a prong fastener/compressor bar mechanism, be sure to understand how the mechanism interacts with the binder covers. Many users, bewilderingly, don't. Stay away from binders from which pages are more likely to fall out, such as clamp fasteners (which also make page turns difficult) and 3-ring binders (which are too bulky and irregular for easy shelving and/or filing).

You can create a *modest* attention-getting cover/title-page layout, if you like, using unusual fonts and type sizes. But keep it simple: avoid illustrations, logos, and paperback-like cover blurbs, which only come off as self-publication and an amateurish cry for attention. You can use subtitles or descriptive enhancements such as: "A New Version for Young Audiences" or "A Murder-Mystery Musical," because they convey hard information and give the reader a quick sense of context and artistic intent. But phrases like "A Laugh-Out-Loud Romantic Farce for the Whole Family!" won't do you any favors, and will probably hurt.

Breakdown Pages

A script should include a page listing a cast of characters thus:

Cast of Characters

BILL PORTER
JACK SUNSHINE
WINIFRED RUBY

If you like, you can enhance these entries *slightly*, e.g., "BILL PORTER, 42, airline executive, black." But don't get into long, psychology-intensive analyses. Nobody reads them, nobody remembers them. The play itself, like any other work of fiction, will take care of portraying the characters for the reader, if it's any good.

You should also have a scene breakdown page. This should include simple basics, such as:

THE TIME:

1950

THE PLACE:

Inner-city Montreal and its environs

and, when applicable, further info, again reduced to basics, such as:

ACT ONE

Scene One: The Porter home, late September, evening
Scene Two: The same, a week later

ACT TWO

Scene One: Porter's office, the next morning
Scene Two: Winifred's nightclub, that afternoon

A musical theatre script should further include a list of "Musical Numbers." The list, if applicable, should be divided by acts. The margins of this page should be justified, with the titles in quotes flush left and the characters who sing flush right, e.g.:

"Angel of Music"   Christine
"New World Order"   M. Richard and Company

Breakdown pages *can* use font styles that are different or bolder or more striking than the font of the play proper—but they don't have to, and again, they should *never* be distractingly fussy or needlessly fancy. When in doubt, always err on the side of conservatism.

Authors' Notes

It's not uncommon for a script to contain a preface consisting of a few paragraphs about its playing style, background, and/or gestation. This is a perfectly legitimate page to include, but take heed—be sure it's *necessary*, be sure it's not *pretentious, pompous,* or *overblown,* and don't confuse it with the synopsis. If it isn't crucial to providing ambiance, point of view, or *brief* historical and/or sociopolitical background, err on the side of caution and leave it out.

Anonymity

Obviously this is not an issue for a straight-ahead producer submission, but some competitions are judged "blind," their rules requesting that scripts, tapes, and such contain no authorship credits. (You'll record your personal info on an application form. The office staff keeps these on file, each one cross-referenced to a project title or an assigned submission number.)

The best thing to do is create *entirely new* title pages, rather than include old pages in which the authorship is crossed out or taped over. Most of the time, these methods don't hide the authors' name(s) sufficiently from view, and in any event, they look bone ugly. You want to provide a neat, businesslike presentation—and remember, the cover and/or the title page is the first thing anyone will see. New labels for any accompanying materials (such as CDs) are also strongly advised.

And for goodness' sake go through the script itself to be sure you don't blow your anonymity within, in a header, a copyright/registry notice, or an author's note. I recently screened a musical script that had a by-the-rules anonymous title page—followed shortly thereafter by a page of authors' bios. This kind of violation not only seems disingenuous . . . it can make you seem just plain stupid.

THE PLAY PROPER

Fonts

The universally "safe" font is twelve-point Courier (the mainstay of the sturdy old IBM Selectric Typewriter, and of services such as Studio Duplicating). Courier is a proportional font (every character uses the same amount of space) and lays out most effectively with an irregular, or "unjustified" right margin. If you want a slightly more elegant desktop publishing look to your script, with *justified* margins, twelve-point Palatino is efficient, attractive, and acceptable. When considering other fonts, keep in mind that they must be neutral and easy on the eyes; and that you may have to adjust the type size, so that the number of pages in the script is not misleading: twelve-point Times New Roman is smaller and more compact than twelve-point Palatino or `twelve-point Courier`. (Naïve writers sometimes try to fit a play they know to be overlong—generally anything over 120 standard pages is edging into the red zone—into the "right" number of pages by reducing the font size of the text. This never fools anybody, and only makes the script look cramped. Better to be forthrightly and honestly lengthy—if you *must*—and hope the play justifies the excess on its own merits.)

Be aware of the cosmetic differences between proportional and nonproportional fonts:

- `where you would use double dashes (--) in Courier -- separated from the words with a space --`
- you would use a single em dash (—) in Palatino—and keep the dash flush with the word.
- `You can use` *`italics`* `or` <u>`underline`</u> `in Courier`
- but you should only use *italics* in Palatino.
- `Double space between sentences in Courier.`
- Single space between sentences in Palatino (remember, it's a publishing font, and takes care of sentence spacing *for* you).

Elements

The basic elements of a playscript are parentheses (long stage directions and shorter internal, or "mid-speech," character directions), character names, dialogue and—in a musical—lyrics. Each begins its own discrete "paragraph" and each is indented differently.

The Placement of Character Names, Dialogue, Parentheses, and Lyrics

In your word-processing program, learn to create what are called "styles" and keystroke commands for them, in order to "wrap" your formats. That way, you won't be constantly deleting white space (from tabs, which are read by the computer as characters) every time you revise a stage direction or a lyric.

Dialogue should be flush left (optional: justified). Lyrics should be indented a half inch or an inch; I prefer the latter (never justify the lyric wrap). Stage directions are a half inch to the right of the lyrics (optional:

justified). Character names, *always* capitalized, can either be computer-centered, like this:

GEORGE   FRANCISCO

MATTHEW   SIKES

GRAZER

—or they can be flush with a center margin, like this:

GEORGE   FRANCISCO

MATTHEW   SIKES

GRAZER

I like to center them, but that's a personal choice. Personal, too, is whether or not they appear in bold print.

There is no double space between a centered character name and the character's speech or lyric.

Internal parentheses should *never* go within the body of the speech (like this); they should be on their own line and indented, thus:

M.   RICHARD

(Looking at the others, dangerously)
"New" season? Did I actually hear the word "new"?
                (Brandishing the handbill disdainfully)
No, ladies and gentlemen. "New" is precisely what *this* is not!

Very long parentheses, scene descriptions, and stage directions that are lengthier than the speech they amplify are similarly indented, and separated from dialogue by a double space.

Lyrics are always typed in caps, to set songs off from dialogue. Thus:

CHARACTER   NAME

THIS IS THE LYRIC
TO THE SONG.
AND ONE MORE SPOT
WHERE CAPS BELONG.

And speaking of caps . . .

Capitalization in Stage Directions

In stage directions, always keep a character's name in capital letters. This lets everybody working on the play know when a character is associated with an activity, so the actors' respective movements and points of focus can be easily tracked.

Even within parentheses, though, the use of caps has rules. For example, here's an incorrect stage direction:

> (PULITZER slowly advances, seating him-
> self beside COCKERILL's desk and away
> from NELLIE on the sofa.)

The uses of PULITZER and NELLIE are correct—because they refer to human beings taking up stage space, whose actions need to be monitored. The use of COCKERILL is not correct. Cockerill is not in action— all his name does in this context is identify the piece of furniture it's attached to; it's irrelevant that he's also in the scene. The use of pronouns in stage directions follows similar rules. HE, SHE, IT (when applicable to a character) and THEY are capitalized because they are indicative of action, for example:

> (HE crosses to his desk, and tosses the
> file over to his colleagues.)

However, possessives and indirect pronouns—*him, her, it, them, his, hers, its, theirs*—are never capitalized, because they are passive in nature. Thus, you would never write:

> (HE crosses to HIS desk, and tosses the
> file over to THEM.)

An ironic discrepancy is that you *might* capitalize thusly:

> (SAM crosses to his desk, and tosses
> the file over to AL and GUSHIE.)

That's because, even though AL and GUSHIE are on the receiving end of the action, they're live bodies onstage, whose names are not being used as modifiers or possessives—and it makes sense to alert the actors playing the roles that a prop will be tossed their way.

Pagination

The page-numbering system is generally three-tiered: Act Number (Roman Numeral) - Scene Number (Arabic) - Act Page Number (Arabic). (Some people make the third tier the *scene* page number, but this is confusing, and a nuisance. Don't go there.) Thus, the eighteenth page of Act Two, scene three, would appear in the upper right corner as:

II-3-18

Like the use of capitals, it's an important reference. Also, quite honestly, an expected courtesy.

One other expected courtesy—avoid submitting scripts printed on both sides of the page. Every page rates a single sheet, with the back of the page left blank.

EXTRAS

Extras are illustrations, supplementary research articles, magazine-like sidebars, scenic designs, ground plans, and so on. The basic rule for these is—avoid them. At best, they indicate that your play can't stand alone. At worst they can make you appear to be loony.

•   •   •   •   •   •   •   •   •

And those are the basics. After that it only has to be good . . .

. . . but you'd be amazed how many points you rack up on appearances. . . .

SCRIPT SAMPLE #1: PUBLISHING FORMAT

(Excerpted from *The Apprenticeship of Duddy Kravitz* book and lyrics by David Spencer, music by Alan Menken)

> *(Lights up on DUDDY, sweaty, disheveled, in waiter outfit, by a serving window. It's morning, and the background babble from the dining room crowd is intense.)*

DUDDY

Paddy, where are my blintzes, I ordered 'em a half hour ago!

> *(IRWIN appears, brushes past DUDDY)*

IRWIN

Four blintzes, Paddy.

> *(HE gets his order immediately, glares at the unseen Paddy. Paddy's hand comes through the window, flips DUDDY the bird. DUDDY runs to another pool of light, the serving window vanishing. Here HE comes to a skidding stop by a middle-aged businessman seated at a table by his middle-aged wife. His name is COHEN.)*

DUDDY

I'm sorry about the blintzes really really sorry it's so backed up in there like you wouldn't believe and—

> *(COHEN holds up a hand for silence. Gets it)*

COHEN

HEY, BOYCHICK.
WHAT'S YOUR NAME —
> *(Squints to read the uniform tag)*

KRAVITZ?
TAKE A BREATH, KRAVITZ.
DON'T BE NERVOUS.
NAME'S COHEN.
HERE FOR THE SEASON.
KNOW WHAT WE GO FOR?
SNAPPY SERVICE.

(Produces a C-note from a pocket)
LOOK: A HUNDRED DOLLAR BILL.
I'M ALWAYS GLAD TO PAY FOR WHAT I GET.
        (Rip)
HALF NOW . . .
        (As HE gives DUDDY half a bill)
AND LATER, IF I'M HAPPY,
NO REASON WE SHOULD SPLIT UP A SET.
CAPEESH?
BUT SHOW ME WHAT YOU'LL DO FOR ME
YET.

        (DUDDY looks over his shoulder toward the serving window, then runs off. COHEN disappears.)

SCRIPT SAMPLE #2: THE SAME, IN COURIER FORMAT

(Lights up on DUDDY, sweaty, disheveled, in
waiter outfit, by a serving window. It's
morning, and the background babble from the
dining-room crowd is intense.)

DUDDY

Paddy, where are my blintzes, I ordered 'em a half hour
ago!

(IRWIN appears, brushes past DUDDY)

IRWIN

Four blintzes, Paddy.

(HE gets his order immediately, glares at the
unseen Paddy. Paddy's hand comes through the
window, flips DUDDY the bird. DUDDY runs to
another pool of light, the serving window
vanishing. Here HE comes to a skidding stop by
a middle-aged businessman seated at a table
by his middle-aged wife. His name is COHEN.)

DUDDY

I'm sorry about the blintzes really really sorry it's
so backed up in there like you wouldn't believe and--

(COHEN holds up a hand for silence. Gets it)

COHEN

HEY, BOYCHICK.
WHAT'S YOUR NAME --
        (Squints to read the uniform tag)
KRAVITZ?
TAKE A BREATH, KRAVITZ.
DON'T BE NERVOUS.
NAME'S COHEN.
HERE FOR THE SEASON.
KNOW WHAT WE GO FOR?

SNAPPY SERVICE.
    (Produces a C-note from a pocket)
LOOK: A HUNDRED-DOLLAR BILL.
I'M ALWAYS GLAD TO PAY FOR WHAT I GET.
    (Rip)
HALF NOW . . .
    (As HE gives DUDDY half a bill)
AND LATER, IF I'M HAPPY,
NO REASON WE SHOULD SPLIT UP A SET.
KAPEESH?
BUT SHOW ME WHAT YOU'LL DO FOR ME
YET.

    (DUDDY looks over his shoulder toward
    the serving window, then runs off.
    COHEN disappears.)

13
CHAPTER

Sound Advice
or:
Demo Recordings

INTRODUCTION: GEE, OUR OLD LASALLE RAN GREAT

You've written a musical, you want to get it "out there." You need to create a representative recording of the score as a selling tool.

Even as recently as the early nineties, if you couldn't budget for pro-studio recording, you'd go into a room with a piano, set up a tape recorder of the best quality you could afford or borrow, and you'd let rip, trying like hell to get the whole thing down in one pass. It generally took at least several takes.

But no matter what, somewhere along the way it was likely that the pianist would flub a chord, the singer would miss a note, a car horn would honk from outside, *some* small glitch or two would wind up on tape, and you'd have to let it be . . . because the performance elements could not be separated and you'd have done the best you could under the circumstances.

And yet, assuming a certain basic degree of all-around proficiency, what you wound up with was *usually* acceptable. To be sure, you would *never* give a producer a tape without performing live for him first; tapes couldn't be trusted to convey theatricality or performance values . . . but for reference, competitions, grant applications, such inexpensively made tapes, and their handwritten packaging, were entirely normal, even respectable. Everyone knew an aspiring musical dramatist was rarely a rich creature.

That leniency is gone. Now such recordings are branded unprofessional. And why?

State of the art, baby. Ears aren't attuned to them anymore, expectations are higher. Think about it: would you be happy if you booted your factory-fresh computer and found a DOS interface running on a Kaypro operating system? How'd you like to be handed the original cast album of your favorite musical . . . on newly minted 78 RPMs?

More than that, many screeners simply don't have the *ability*, let alone the willingness, to discern the quality of a roughly recorded score; less discerning ears *literally* wouldn't get their bearings on even a simple melody.

Yesterday's innovation is tomorrow's inconvenience. And you have no choice but to deal with it.

Dealing

First off, come to grips with this: you're going to spend a coupla bucks.

Earn it, steal it, borrow it, pull it out of your savings. But resign yourself to it.

Demo recordings have in large measure *supplanted* live auditions. The visionary, imaginative mavens—the Merricks, the Ostrows, the Saint Subbers—who once brute-forced a production into being through sheer pioneer will, have in large measure given way to moonlighting real-estate moguls, consortiums, corporations, movie studios, and other groups. Demos get passed around, discussed, debated, filed, memo'd, second-guessed, *and you never know what level of person will be listening*: a hired-help screener, or the honcho who can green-light the project. So the demo has to grab 'em on *first listening*. They have to *want to pass it on, with no fear of having their judgment questioned.* And yes, production values *count!* Imagine a sea of musicals seeking production, most of them sinking slowly, slowly to the inky-dark bottom. That CD is your show's best flotation device.

PRESENTATION

Note, I said CD. Cassettes have fallen out of favor. Why? Because fast-forwarding and rewinding are linear, repetitive, time-consuming, boring, *irritating* tasks.

If a screener has to quick-scan through a lot of garbage on a particular reel to get to the gem some misguided writer may have buried in the middle of side A, the chances are good that the gem will go unheard . . . and *certain* that the screener will resent waiting while the capstans torture their way through revolution after revolution.

A CD lets the listener skip around at will, which gives you a better shot, and get a fairer listening. (As for those very few places that still *ask* for cassettes, that will change, imminently. Create demos on CDs and dub cassette copies as needed.)

Just as anything less than a professionally presented libretto can sabotage the way your work is perceived, an ill-conceived demo is usually a death sentence. And the packaging can be almost as vital as the recording.

Unlike script formatting, demo presentation is not a wholly standardized affair—there's a margin for personal variation. What you're getting here is specific to *my* approach. So if you find that it's not practical to follow the advice herein *to the letter,* adapt its general guiding principles to your needs.

And now, to better promote clean demos, a little dissertation on—

Garbage

I referred to it before. Speaking demo-wise, what *is* garbage?

Garbage is anything extraneous. Garbage is what a screener or a producer should *not* have to be listening to or wading through between better tracks. Garbage is material that makes the listener suspect a lack of professionalism.

Garbage is the enemy.

The most common manifestation of garbage is the overture. The very notion of an overture on a demo denotes pretension at worst, naïveté at best. The overture is the *last* thing ever written for a show because, as common sense would indicate, *that's* when you know which of the many, possibly dozens, of songs you've written are actually *remaining in the score.* The same applies to dance music or extended passages of incidental music: unless you're in production, working in tandem with designers, a director, and a choreographer, you can have no *idea* what the practical requirements of such music may be. Writing it in advance is folly. Presenting it as part of a preliminary vision is goofy. It's almost impossible for a demo submission to recover from that.

Also avoid excessive narration. In general, I'd say avoid narration of any sort, but *occasionally,* depending upon the style of your demo, *some* narration may be necessary, and helpful. As a rule, demos that provide interpolated continuity (linking material between or within numbers) should be those in which the authors perform their own work, because author-performance demos can approximate the ambience of a live

audition (as opposed to full-cast demos, wherein narrative can only violate verisimilitude—unless narrative is a pre-existing theatrical device
that is an actual component of the show's libretto).

Here's a list of other garbage to avoid:

- **Apologias, editorial comments, and/or excuses.** I once heard a
tape in which some old coot, with what I suppose he took to be
avuncular good humor, announced his hope that the listener
wouldn't mind his inability to play piano; his dream being that
the score would be arranged, harmonized, and notated in production. Whereby he proceeded to whistle, hum, and sing a cappella.
You can measure the length of time a screener will stick with a
demo like this in *seconds*.

- **Lyricless music.** There are actually people out there—a *lot* of
them—who send demos of nothing but accompaniment and
melody lines, fully expecting the listener to follow along with the
script and match the words to the notes.

- **Bad recordings of live performances.** Unless you can record an
expertly rendered and theatrically exciting live performance through
a versatile enough in-house sound system to give you a good mix,
these demos can be self-defeating, and the live-audience reaction
off-putting.

And now that we've covered what to avoid, let's look at the things to
work *toward*.

Judgment Calls

There are different schools of thought about what makes the best kind of
demo. Two of the most common urban legends are (1) that orchestrated
demos are trying to hide something: if the score can't be communicated
effectively via piano, it can't be very good; and (2) that generic vocal performances are better than stellar, as they provide leeway for the imagination of directors and producers to envision things for themselves—if it's
too idiosyncratically "performed" (the theory goes), the listening
honchos will feel that they've been given no room to contribute, and will
be less likely to take on the project.

My personal feeling about this is—you can't be responsible for the
prejudice of somebody else, nor for second-guessing a preconditioned
reaction; you can only be responsible for creating the best product within
your capability. As MIDI-generated music has become more and more per-

vasive, the piano-only philosophy has been rendered increasingly obsolete. I know a number of *brilliant* theatre composers who believe that there is some music that simply isn't presented in its best light when rendered solely on piano. The instrumental approach depends entirely upon what the composer is trying to accomplish. (Personally, I happen to *think* in orchestral colors, and I can't play a decent piano lick to save my life; so my demos are *only* orchestrated, because I have no other choice. And thus far they've won several awards and grants for me.) As for "generic vocal performances" . . . if you think your demo can survive them, it's your call. All I can tell you is, I want *my* demos to sound like polished cast albums, or as near to that as practicality allows. Communicating theatricality is half the game, and if your score can be spectacularly acted and sung, why waste the effort on anything less?

All that said, demos that use nothing but piano accompaniment are *perfectly fine*—as are demos in which the authors present their own work. But it is vital that the pianist be a dramatically sensitive, technically exacting musician—and if the authors sing their own work, *they must be able to sell it.* "Sell it" doesn't necessarily mean sing like a boid—it means you can gratifyingly deliver the intent, get the right message across, make it compelling. If you're an author with a voice that is bad, croaky, imprecise of pitch, self-conscious when acting, wobbly, or otherwise unlikely to inspire confidence, bag the idea of doing it yourself. You won't do your work any favors, and your chutzpah will not be admired. On the other hand, *expert* author-performance demos can generate a rare excitement.

Similarly, if you're using actors, take the time to cast the demo memorably and well. If you don't have a roster of *first-rate* people to call upon (avoid family and subpar college colleagues), don't be too shy or intimidated to ask around: that kind of networking is part of what working in the theatre is about. You'll develop a reliable roster in time; and—I promise you—as long as your deportment is professional and considerate, you'll be flabbergasted at the quality, and frequently the identities, of the performers who'll say *yes*.

Demo Types

There are four kinds of theatrical demo.

1. **The Full-Score Preproduction Demo:** Exactly as the name implies, a recording of whatever complete draft you want to send out to elicit interest in your show. This can be a composite of individual recordings you've made throughout the creative

process, or a wholly new demo. The drawback to the "anthology" approach is the likelihood of inconsistency: unforeseen circumstances may necessitate your changing actors in midstream for one role or another; or, due to revisions, earlier recordings may not match the accompanying script once it has sustained cuts, refinements, additions, and other changes. (If your demos are produced in a home studio, there are possible technical solutions to some of these issues, and I'll cover that later.) If the presentation is attractive, polished, and professional, and if the inconsistencies aren't *too* distracting, you're probably in good shape with a composite selection of tracks. But if you're even *slightly* in doubt, or aspire to the ideal, start from scratch and do it over. Approach it like an album, so it's all clearly of the same sensibility and fabric.

2. **The Postproduction Demo:** The recording of the score you make—if you have to—*after* a full production. This can be in lieu of, in anticipation of, or by way of securing a cast album. Failing the existence of an actual cast album, the postproduction demo can be crucial to placing your musical with a stock-and-amateur licensing organization. Copies of the demo can subsequently be the audio selling tool the licensers routinely send out with perusal scripts. (Since the postproduction demo is a permanent record of a *finished* and *produced* score, it may well include some purely instrumental tracks—such as overtures—that seem appropriate.)

   If you're unsure of your show's future prospects, and *especially* if the show proved itself an audience pleaser, *never* let the opportunity to record the score, while the performers and musicians still know it freshly, pass by, *even* if it means footing the bill yourself and cutting a deal with one of the record producers who specialize in distributing such material. The expense will pay for itself down the line.

3. **The Sampler:** This is a *selection* of songs, and it varies with need. Submission requirements sometimes limit you to a certain number of representative songs or minutes—and some writers find it useful to have a multipurpose "highlights" CD on hand. But whether you create the demo to specifications or assemble existing tracks, bear in mind what the recording needs to accomplish.

In *most* cases, your few numbers should each need little or no setup to be understood and emphasize *dramatic highlights* of the piece. A beautifully arranged choral number may not matter worth diddly if the listener is not interested in the character singing, or not getting some *sense* of story. Be sure as well to demonstrate a range of song types: comedy songs, ballads, charm songs, musical scenes (if not too complex).

Similarly, *beware including music that may be too sophisticated or "artsy" for an untrained, slow, or casual ear.* Said music may be every bit as breathtaking as you think it is; but if it doesn't communicate outside the full-show or full-score environment, it is *not* your friend on a sampler. When in doubt, try it out on colleagues and friends.

And whatever the published guidelines you're provided for submitting your sampler, *follow them precisely . . .* or, at any rate, as precisely as your applicable material permits.

4. **The Maintainer:** Once your show is in development, it sometimes behooves you to keep a "running tab" that reflects changes in the score, to provide concerned personnel with updated reference material. Interim adjustments can usually be handled in a quick-and-dirty fashion: the mix needn't be perfect, and the author(s) singing the material should be fine. However, if at any point the demo is required to speak to "outsiders" for the impending production, then you need to overhaul, and recapture the polish of your initial presentation. The good news, at least in commercial venues, is that if your producers are in earnest, they'll cover the cost of new recording as a production expense.

CD Packaging

With scanners and color printers being so inexpensive and pervasive, it's easier than ever to create fancy graphics and distinctive logos for CD jewel boxes right in your own home. But remember that they're worse than useless unless implemented *very* tastefully.

Keep the presentation to the point; choose or create designs and fonts that evoke the essence of the show with simple elegance, and be sure title and authorship, which belong on that front panel, can "interact" with the design such that they're displayed with due prominence and appropriateness. And bear in mind, too, nothing's wrong with keeping to an intelligent layout of basic text. (Obviously, with regard to competitions where the rules require you to submit material anonymously, you reconfigure and edit this info as common sense dictates.)

There are two kinds of jewel cases, standard and slim. Each has its storage advantages and neither is particularly preferable over the other. A slim case can slide easily into a pocket on the script's inside front cover; whereas a standard case has two spines for title-author info, which allows the demo to be easily retrieved from a stack of other cased CDs.

Standard offers you more flexibility of design and information display. The CD holder snaps out of a transparent tray that holds a U-card (sometimes erroneously called a J-card, a holdover from cassette terminology) and that gives you the freedom to put your track and cast listings, plus agent/contact info, on the rear of the case. The advantage here is that all the basic data is visible at first glance. Thus the front insert can be either a four-panel booklet, in which panels two, three, and four contain a story synopsis (not dry or dull, but *concise*), and/or author bios; or a simple two-panel card with perhaps a brief, tasteful description of the project and/or bio info on panel two.

A slim jewel case requires more economy of presentation, as its CD holder is a single plastic piece that doubles as the case rear and doesn't accommodate U-cards. Thus you're limited to a front insert whose first panel has to display not only title and authorship, but contact info as well; the first panel, remember, is the only one in plain view when the jewel case is shut—and you never want anybody in a position to move your work forward to have to hunt for vital information. If you want your slim-case insert to be a four-panel booklet, with cover design, only the two inner panels can hold explanatory text. You'll need the fourth panel for lists, because that quick-reference data should be visible as soon as the jewel case is opened.

The label on the actual disk should clearly duplicate the project title, authorship, and contact info. (Learn to create and use text boxes and tables in your word-processing program, which allow precise positioning of info without your having to go through contortions trying to get the tab key and space bar to manipulate a stable, balanced-looking layout.) Resist the temptation to have the CD label display nothing but a graphic, or only graphic and title. Remember, if the CD itself is ever separated from its jewel case and inserts, your vital info needs to remain accessible.

The CD label I created for copies I burn of the original *Weird Romance* cast album, which is currently out of print, is shown in Figure 1.

Figure 1. CD Label

Cassette Packaging

Fading medium though it is, the cassette tape is still occasionally re-quested (at this writing, the Guggenheim Fellowship Application still, oddly, insists on cassettes). Packaging here is a more conservative business.

Don't bother with graphics; they take up too great a proportion of the *very* limited amount of printable "real estate" that *should* be devoted to the vital info detailed above, plus side A/side B track orders.

A demo cassette's printable real estate has two parts.

The first is the J-card insert for the cassette case, named for the letter it resembles when viewed in cross-section. It has three subdivisions: from top to bottom, the backflap, the spine, and the frontspiece.

In my cassette days, I used the backflap for my agent's name and ad-dress, and the spine for the title of the project and the authorship. The face panel *reiterated* title and authorship, and under that, provided the remaining information. To keep it all from seeming *too* bland, I allowed myself a modestly fancy title font and pastel-colored paper.

Figure 2 shows one of my standard templates for the J-card layout for a nonexistent musical's postproduction demo—with outlines added to articulate the sections.

The second part of a cassette's printable real estate is the one or two adhesive labels (depending on how many sides you use) that go on the physical cassette. You won't lose points for hand-writing clearly on the slim crack-and-peel labels that come with brand-name blanks; but it's nicer—and recommended—to print out professional-looking, full-size labels.

The label need not duplicate all the information on the J-card; in fact, a clean, uncluttered presentation is preferable. See Figure 3 for the label on the first side of the same *Usual Suspects* demo.

Representative for Tune Smith: The Tough Negotiator Company. Limited
340 West 55th Street / New York, NY 10019 / (212) 555-7614

The Usual Suspects
Music and Lyrics by **Tune Smith**   Book by **Fellow Scribe**

The Original Off-Broadway Cast in
The Usual Suspects
...a noir musical...
Book and Direction by FELLOW SCRIBE
Music. Lyrics and Orchestrations by TUNE SMITH

Angel Dunne **Jenny Reiger**   Joe Pockets **John Wallyhood**
Grifter **Kenneth Boydon**   Bluejaw McCain **Craig Oldfeather**
Mrs. Berg **Jean Reltaf** Carlotta **Nicole Salmon** Bunky **Michael Princeton**

Side A
Prologue & Misdemeanor
Throwin' the Book at You, Baby!
The Big Score (incidental)
A Bag Marked Swag
Counterfeit Angel
Fingerprints on My Heart
Ali-bye-bye
She Read Me My Rights
Who's Miranda? (incidental)

Side B
Fugue for Tin Ears
Your Safe's With Me (incidental)
Cuff Him? I Don't Even *Know* Him!
A Kind Word and a Gun
I'm da PD, He's da DA
Plastique Love
My Man (on the Upper Bunk)
Chalk Outline Cha-Cha (Finale)
Bow Music

Figure 2. J-card layout

Figure 3. Cassette label

Never forget, the packaging of your demo is the first thing a screener sees. The more assured the presentation, the more likely the listener is likely to feel in good hands. After that what's on the inside has merely to live up to what's on the outside . . .

And that brings us to—

TECHNICAL CONSIDERATIONS

Now we get to the hard-core stuff: How you make the recording in the first place, and under what professional conditions.

What follows will *usually* be the purview of composers or composer/lyricists and not be the *hands-on* responsibility of dedicated wordsmiths. You wordsmiths, though, *absorb what you can.* Skim if you must, but get a *general* idea of the technical options so that you can assess them properly with your composer, if you're starting from scratch. If you're working with a composer who already has recording experience, so much the better. This will give you an insight into what she has to deal with.

To you composers, here's where the elements that make or break a demo's capacity for sounding professional and compelling are largely in your hands.

Expenses

The accepted rule is that each discipline—book, music, lyrics—is responsible for a third of any project's demo cost, for example, actors, pro-studio time (if applicable), and material. If you wear two hats, you pay two-thirds, since when royalties come in, you make two-thirds of the money. Shared expenses usually do *not* apply to *recording hardware;* a lyricist wouldn't chip in for his composer's home-studio setup any more than the composer would contribute to the lyricist's computer, as such gear is an expected part of the individual artist's basic toolkit, and gets used project after project. (Although a team exclusive to each other may *well* share hardware expenses, as the team benefit is continuous from project to project.)

Where You Record

There are two venues where your money can be spent.

The first is a pro recording studio. This can be a commercial outfit or a privately owned home studio, which may do double duty as a money-making part of a composer/arranger's personal setup.

Either way, you're usually into the studio management for a *minimum* of fifty bucks an hour. This includes not just recording time, but mixing and mastering time as well.

Beware the hidden limitation: even if the studio has state-of-the-art capability, you must make sure that your accompanists and vocalists are rehearsed to within an inch of their lives. Rest assured, you'll do multiple takes *anyway* . . . but you don't want to be adding them to your clock time as a consequence of the material not being sufficiently learned. Your job is a little easier if the accompaniments (say, MIDI orchestrations played by a synthesizer) are already recorded. You'll pay for the time it takes the studio to transfer those tracks to in-house equipment, but your only unpredictable expense will be overdubbing vocals.

The cost of any portable recording medium the studio dedicates or distributes, such as CDs, DVDs, ADAT reels, DAT tape, or even analog cassettes is also provided by you.

So *budget carefully and liberally!* Prepare to exceed your ideal estimate. Sit in on a studio session or two that you're *not* involved with—to get a sense of the available "toys" plus the recording and mixing processes.

A recording studio is hardly the most cost-efficient way to go. Over time, perhaps even per project, you will far exceed the price of doing it yourself.

Yet if you're *absolutely certain* the recording studio is your method of choice—because you like having expert technicians on hand; or you're too incurably technophobic to deal—you may choose to skip what follows and go right to the subsection called "Flesh-Tech."

But for those interested in optimum control and the most versatile, re-usable, long-range bang for the buck, the second option is the best: your own home studio setup. Your time is your own to control, the gear usually pays for itself after the first demo, you can do all the work without ever leaving your living space, and if you get into multitracking, scheduling singers is a breeze—because you can lay down separate instrumentals and vocals, build a recording like a mosaic, and produce a finished result that sounds like all the performers were in the same room at the same time. Vocals, too, can be recorded in increments—the need for that one perfect take has vanished like Edison's wax cylinders.

You'll need a few obvious things: stereo amplifier, headphones, microphones, cables, and speakers. The big question is what recording station they hook into.

You have a wide range of product possibilities within four categories: *high-tech, intermediate-tech, mid-tech, low-tech.* The operative word, however, is *tech.* Whatever route you travel, the end result needs to be a demo that sounds clean and professional. It needn't be studio-pristine, but it needs to be tastefully conceived, have "present" fidelity, and demonstrate at least rudimentary pro-recording savvy.

Two more cautions:

1. Whatever "tech" your budget allows, *do your homework and purchase only the best equipment in that range.* If you settle for cheap dreck, you'll quickly discover you've made a costly bargain.

2. Even if you eventually buy from an out-of-state mail order place (no tax, and *they* deliver), go to your local music gear store anyway. Speak to the salespeople as if you *intend* them to make a commission off you (relax: you're not the only one doing it, and they know it's an occupational hazard) and take *long, hard, lingering looks* at the "toys" you're thinking about. For you want, as much as possible, to make sure their interfaces and control panels are intuitive: easy to understand, figure out, experiment with, negotiate, and operate. Remember—the ultimate goal is to spend time doing your work, not puzzling over the equipment.

How You Record

High-Tech. . . . is the most powerful and versatile way to go, the terrain of digital recording, ideally right onto a hard drive. "Digital" means just that—the sound is recorded as a numeric code, and stored as computer data. When played back, it is read and processed by an electronic scanner (e.g., the laser in a CD player). Because this scanner *never comes*

*into physical contact with the storage medium, the once-common surface noise or
"hiss" of analog media (regular cassettes and vinyl) is completely eliminated.*

Digital *recording* also means nondestructive *editing.* If you splice or
erase a tape, you irrevocably alter the available information. But anything saved digitally can always be retrieved and reconsidered.

High-tech digital recording additionally allows sound to be manipulated the way text is manipulated in a word processor:

- Pitch, timbre, and entire keys can be adjusted, not just on MIDI
  tracks, but on *vocals!*
- The timing of entrances can be corrected by sliding them over; cut/
  copy/paste functionality can be achieved with a computer
  keystroke, or a few ministudio controller moves.
- High-tech automates your mix, allowing your changing settings to
  be made with pinpoint dynamic precision, freeing you of manually manipulating knobs and sliders as you listen to playback
  while you work, and/or do your final mixdown.
- You can composite an ideal vocal performance by connecting the
  best excerpts from multiple takes—while preserving the illusion
  that it was all done in one spontaneous go.
- And you can store as many composites as you desire, give yourself
  as many options as possible, as well as the freedom to experiment.
- Usually too, with both software studios and ministudios, desired
  "effects" such as reverb are on-board, so there's no need to purchase a separate effects processor.

In short, high-tech offers almost limitless production power, while
yielding recordings whose technical and artistic sophistication can render them indistinguishable in quality from commercially released pro-
studio material.

To enter this realm, you need either the aforementioned computer-
driven software studio or a dedicated recorder-mixer, a.k.a. a mini-studio.

A software studio, as the name implies, means you're using a computer
program and storing recording data to a hard drive. It requires having
enough hard-drive space available for the task (recording data needs a
lot of it); and you will also need interface hardware that will translate
audio signals from mics and other inputs into digital information of professional quality.

One of the most compelling features of a software studio is endless expandability: as new versions of, and plug-ins to, the various programs are written, functions and operations become more numerous and more versatile. For maintaining state-of-the-art flexibility and operational ease, the software studio is your best bet.

A digital mini-studio recorder-mixer—provided it's a full-feature model (see *Intermediate Tech,* following)—does the same job and produces results that are indistinguishable from computer-generated recordings. These "boxes" (sometimes called "workstations") are dedicated units— rather than *running* a program, they *are* the program, and they're governed by a combination of operating system software and machine-running *firm*ware, so-called because, distinct from *soft*ware, it constitutes a nonremovable, wholly proprietary program on a nonremovable drive; a drive that is separate from the *removable* drive that holds your work files (data). Mini-studios are a little more complex and time-consuming to learn and use than software studios, and slower because they're more mechanical, but their data-storage drives are swappable, and they come with sufficient space for your active work. The necessary sound-converters are built in, and there's a lot to be said for avoiding the system conflicts and file corruption that infrequently but potentially plague computer recording.

There are, however, three drawbacks to consider where mini-studios are concerned:

1. **Except for the most expensive models, built-in screen interfaces tend to be small, measurable in one-digit inches.** By contrast, a software studio would fill any size monitor with a full, color display that includes easy access to data windows plus a complement of clickable menus and toolbars. A mini-studio display tends (at this writing) to be monochrome or grayscale, and requires paging through multiple hidden views to get at information needed for precision editing. Plus, the physical panel requires the mastery of multifunction buttons, knobs, dials, and faders. On the upside: Many of these units can be "slaved" to a computer, to be controlled within standard music sequencing programs, giving you both a dedicated box *and* a full-screen computer interface—*if* you don't mind storing each song's mixing data in files on the computer. (At this writing, mini-studios can't function as auxiliary hard drives.)

2. **Operating system updates are finite.** Occasional software updates (usually downloadable from the manufacturer's Internet site) do install a little versatility and refinement to existing functions. But those functions are linked to an unyielding and unchangeable set of physical parts, so the firmware basics can never be rewritten, remapped, or renovated. On the upside: Digital sound information is digital sound information; even if it takes a few more steps on an older box, *you can still manipulate it as needed.* The sole advantage to updating your firmware (or trading up to a perkier model) is added operational convenience.

3. **There's a physical limit to the number of tracks you can use at one time** (whereas a software studio lets you create unlimited tracks at will). On the upside: This is only a logistical problem, not an artistic one. Let's say you have an eight-track box but need to record ten vocals, and you need another two tracks for instrumental. Each of the eight tracks will have at least eight levels for alternate takes and/or storage of additional information. And you can "bounce" (combine) tracks as you build your stereo mix (which ultimately of course feeds into only two channels anyway) such that all the voices you need are available to you for the final result. So long as you store pristine versions of the info before you combine it, you can always go back to the drawing board.

   And on a personal note, I use a sixteen-track digital mini-studio which has *never* disappointed me.

Whatever your medium, computer or mini-studio, there's another astonishing feature digital high-tech offers: every musical goes through several development drafts, existing songs get revised, and if the revisions are significant, a new demo needs to reflect that. But if you routinely allocate separate tracks to all your performance elements, *you have the ability to update and edit prior recordings!* This includes cleaning up and remixing recordings from analog tape masters; revising performances; replacing performers; conjoining retainable sections of older recordings seamlessly with newly created and recorded sections; and just about any other "magical" editing trick you can imagine.

This kind of flexibility should not be underestimated (especially where lengthy and/or production numbers are concerned). And it beats the time/cost limitations of the pro-studio process hands down.

Intermediate-Tech. A *very* recent (and inevitable) development is that music gear manufacturers have begun offering low-cost digital recorders (i.e., under $500) that have eight tracks or less, smaller hard-drive capacity, and *limited* functionality—the most significant omission being automated mixing. But they allow you to perform many of the editing tricks of the fancier units. So be *very* certain of any model's capacity before you buy. In short order these will probably phase out analog recording altogether, but for now these budget-minded boxes are a compromise between *high tech* and—

Mid-Tech. . . . which again, tends to involve analog tape—reel-to-reel or cassette, but the latter is easier.

With the understanding that the demos you make will be distributed on CD, it doesn't matter that your master recording is done to tape. If a mid-tech mini-studio is what you have and/or all you can afford, no one needs to know *how* you recorded, so long as the end result is professional and pleasing. And while tape usually does not allow you to automate your mixing choices, and it renders electronic data manipulation an impossible fantasy, it still gives you multitrack flexibility and creates a damned impressive product.

In this realm it's best to acquire a max-capacity eight-channel recorder-mixer. Cassette mini-studios use common high-bias analog cassettes as the recording medium, but record at an accelerated speed and the tape heads, miraculously, subdivide that little strip of tape into *eight discrete tracks of stunningly high fidelity!* And the transport controls are hair-trigger.

You can bounce tracks as you would on a digital box. The drawback is that when you combine tracks thus, you compound tape hiss. Nor can you change your mind and *undo* a procedure as you can digitally. All such edits, on tape, are called "destructive" because they forever alter the source material. Prepare also for the process of mixing the old way: memorizing your tracks, rehearsing your moves, and manipulating faders/knobs/buttons manually. You'll probably do several passes on each number before creating the mix you want for your master. Where longer numbers with convenient musical rests are concerned, you may find that your master pass derives from a composite. And as you mix, you'll want to disable tracks that are blank for any significant length of time, because keeping an "empty pot" open adds that track's tape hiss to the final mix.

Because cassette mini-studios do *not* have on-board processors and effects, you'll also need the following:

- **An effects box**—primarily for reverb, though other effects, like echo, can have dramatic uses too. (Reverb, it pays to note, though, is no longer standard currency on demos *or* cast albums. These days many feature a "dry" sound. How much reverb you use, if any, is a judgment call, but no-frills effects boxes are cheap and give you the option.)
- **A pro-quality recorder to receive your stereo mixdowns,** preferably a digital recorder for a positive, exact "capture," though a very high-end analog tape unit will serve with no analog-to-analog-dub generation loss of any consequence.
- **A medium for mastering**—that is, assembling all the mixed songs in demo order, putting the proper spaces between them, setting a uniform sound level and creating a master copyable CD, a burnable CD disk image, or, as a last resort, a master cassette from which you will dub your copies. This doesn't have to be anything fancy: a computer with basic sound-input software, a CD recorder, or a decent tape deck with a hair-trigger pause button (such as the venerable Sony Professional Walkman).

Low-Tech. . . . is almost identical to mid-tech in procedure . . . but it's much less expensive and much more limited. Low-tech makes use of porta[ble]-studios. They are analog tape recorder-mixers, priced in the low-to-mid hundreds, that allow you only four (in rare cases six) tracks to work with, but if you don't mind restricting your number of vocals, and favor live piano tracks, they can be reasonably efficient—and they do allow geographical freedom in choosing where to record. There are even *lower*-priced porta-studios that feature *fewer* than four tracks, but before you go that route, I'd recommend you just take a flying leap off a high building: it's a cheaper, faster way to end your career.

Tips for All Tech

Whatever your tech preference, a note that applies to all.

Never filter vocals through effects processors when you record. Always record the vocals "dry." You can't remove or adjust a pre-recorded effect if it proves unsatisfactory in the mix. However, when you apply effects as *filters* through which dry vocals pass on their way to a final L-R stereo mixdown, you can always rethink your choices and try again.

Instrumental accompaniments generated by MIDI synthesizers may need to be handled differently. If you have a kick-ass computer-based studio with a huge mixing board and several synths, you have maximum mixing flexibility and can "ride" each instrumental patch separately. But if (like me) you have to dump a wholly pre-mixed track to a mini-studio, it *can* be fully processed (some all-purpose synths have on-board effects). So long as the track is well conceived, it will hold up fine as you overdub vocals and make general volume adjustments for balance.

Flesh-Tech: Budgeting for Auxiliary Humans

If you're going to use actors on your demos, you're going to have to pay them. If they're good friends who insist upon doing you a favor—insist more strongly than *they* do that they *take the dough.* This is vitally important, not just because it's a nod to professional etiquette, but because it has *direct* bearing on your technical needs. No matter *how* much tech flexibility you have, you can't turn *bad* raw data into *good*. If the vocal track you're left with at the end of the day isn't satisfying, you've labored for naught. Rule to live by: tiring actors who haven't been paid, or don't expect to be, are less likely to give their all, or even remain wholly patient, as the takes mount up. Conversely, actors who know you appreciate their professionalism enough to pay for it will strive—sometimes unrealistically—to prove their inexhaustibility. And loyalty. (Don't forget, they're investing in *you*, too.)

For a quick session that doesn't require much time—say, a backup vocal or something short and unchallenging—fifty to seventy-five dollars is not unreasonable; for an extended session, detailed character work, etc.: one hundred dollars or higher. I have my own personal formulæ for working this out—as you will have yours—and different circumstances (and personnel) demand different solutions; the dollar amount is less important than the psychological health generated by the gesture.

Be on the alert for vocal fatigue that a simple time-out won't alleviate; recognize the moment when you have to let the actor off the hook and stop for the day, even unfinished . . . and, consequently, prepare for the advent of a second *paid* session: frequently, the songs you think will be the hardest to lay down will be the easiest—and vice versa. Understand that recording a demo is an *entirely different process* than rehearsing for live presentation, requiring *different* use of the muscles and *different* concentration.

Allow yourself a "petty cash" cushion for food, drink, and other unforseeables. And bonuses—e.g., for staying "way after class"—or for the loyal actor who isn't feeling well, but shows up anyway because he knows you're on a deadline; as well as cab fare to send that same actor home with minimal added discomfort.

Petty cash should also provide for your own inadvertent screw-ups. For example: sometimes, with the best of intentions, you'll unwittingly hire the wrong, or an inadequate, actor. No matter: if she's working hard and prepared, she gets the full fee—*even as you already know you're going to replace her voice with another.* Whether or not you go through the motions of finishing the session is a judgment call. It's worth it to be sensitive. (Should you wind up hiring a slacker, pay a fairish minimum for the effort of showing up—if the fee hasn't been agreed upon in advance, that is, otherwise you're stuck—and don't rehire that person.)

Make sure the music you hand out is clean, clear, presentable, and easy to study (giving it to them well in advance, with reference CDs or tapes, is also a good idea); and see that the environment in which you record—be it an apartment or a pro studio—somehow encourages comfort and enthusiasm. You won't get optimum results in a cramped or depressing space, or with an even mildly ungenerous attitude.

Some degrees of dry-running, rehearsing, coaching—and schmoozing—are unavoidable. As a general rule, allow two hours to record a simple number, four for a complex one. If your song requires more than one vocalist and you record each voice individually, the formula must be applied *per performer.*

With appropriate variations, the above applies to hired accompanists, too. If said accompanists are also used as arrangers to help you shape a "hummer" score, be sure to work out a clear, formal financial arrangement that indemnifies you in creative matters, while keeping the accompanist on your side.

The performance personnel expenditure for an *average full-score* demo, using a cast of six or more, can be budgeted in the area of one thousand dollars. You may not go near that high; you may go higher. But a thousand is a safe, rough estimate. (Demoing individual songs varies according to circumstance.)

Think of the human factor as the last installation of hardware in the technical chain. And remember, people require maintenance and sensitivity as vigilant as that which you'd lavish on *any* delicate equipment.

Two Final CD Cautions

1. Everyone knows you can purchase blank CDs in bulk, but be careful which brand you choose. Some render inconsistent results and may not play well on older CD players. Since you have no knowledge of what machine a producer, director, screener, colleague, or loved one will be using, *spend the few extra bucks.* Once you find a brand or two that work for you—stick. What you don't save on money you'll save on aggravation and uncertainty.

2. Whenever your CD-demo is going someplace important—a producer, a competition, a high-profile director—do yourself a favor and proof-listen the disc *all the way through,* on the *oldest* CD player you own, before sending it out. Even with a good brand of CD, you can inadvertently burn that rare copy with skips and dropouts. Several years ago, a proof-listening saved me from sending a "coaster" to the Rodgers competition—which I *won,* just so you understand how crucial this can be—and the near miss is still a harrowing memory.

SAVING MONEY ON LABELS AND INSERTS

While, as I say, you can never, *and must never try to,* stint on *electronic* quality, there are certain *nontechnical* budgetary expenses that can be kept lower than "the man" wants you to think.

If you've priced labels and inserts, you're painfully aware that paper vendors gleefully expect you to bleed out of your wallet for them—the consumer cost for even a year's supply can be absurd. Yet how can you *avoid* paying thirty dollars or more for a box of twenty-five to fifty sheets and *still* have good-looking presentations that don't require you to spend precious do-it-yourself hours with a ruler and scissors?

Answer: You change the rules of the game.

Step 1: Go forth and download. Ironically, all the major paper product vendors (Avery, Fellowes/Neato, CD Stomper, and others) furnish you with some of the basic ammo to cut costs, *right off their own websites:* Free, downloadable template files. Entire comprehensive sets of them. For CDs, cassettes, cases, the works. Compatible with most word-processing and desktop-publishing programs and even a few commonly used graphics programs.

Their files display borders around and guidelines within each pattern, aligned to conform with the articulated sheets you are meant to buy.

Using them, you set text and graphics within correctly measured fields; and once that's done, you "invisify" or delete them (usually with a preset keystroke), leaving only your finished design, for a neat job of printing.

Now: let's consider our options with the two *categories* of paper goods for which we've downloaded our free templates in the first place—*adhesive* paper products and *nonadhesive* paper products.

Adhesive Paper Products

Because adhesive paper products—specifically CD and cassette labels—aren't the kind of thing most of us can create neatly out of raw materials, you do have to buy them. But a little diligent web-browsing will turn up vendors that sell in quantity at discount prices.

Step 2: Locate such a vendor and make it your source. The best place I've found so far is Lin-Pak Division, P.O. Box 88, Swanton, Ohio, toll free: (800) 524-4845, phone: (419) 826-9977, fax: (419) 826-9978, email: Sales@linpak.com, website: www.linpak.com.

Lin-Pak makes and/or distributes label sheets that use the standard brand-name layouts for their templates. You choose the pattern you need. The paper is a little thinner, but the resulting labels are just as good, and the savings are significant. Where you might pay fifteen dollars or so for a box of fifty CD labels at Comp-USA or Staples, twenty-five dollars gets you a box of two hundred from Lin-Pak. For a little more money, custom features, like color, are also available.

Nonadhesive Paper Products

These are the inserts for J-cards, tray-cards, and booklets that display information through the plastic cases of CDs and cassettes. The perforated, heavy-stock sheets you can buy are certainly a convenience . . . but if you're willing to be only *slightly* industrious—figure an extra fifteen to thirty minutes for each presentation—you can eschew these and cut the cost of your supplies by at least 90 percent.

Step 3: Buy a paper trimmer. All office supply vendors have 'em. It's a tool with a flat surface (often displaying an alignment grid), some form of paper guide/safety guard mechanism—and either a hinged, tension-spring blade-arm or an enclosed rotary blade that operates along a straight track. The trimmer is the most expensive thing you'll buy for your insert-making setup—between approximately thirty-five dollars and one hundred and twenty dollars, depending upon how wide a surface you want to work on and how sturdily built the trimmer is—but unlike paper, it's a permanent piece of equipment which you only pay for *once*.

Step 4: Choose your blank paper. You can use regular 8½ x 11 inch bond of any color, or the slightly heavier card stock that paper supply vendors use for their perforated sheets. (Before buying heavier stock, though, be sure you know the maximum thickness your printer can handle.)

Step 5: Go to your computer and boot the application in which you intend to do your design work.

Step 6: Select an applicable template, generate a new document, and create your design. For the sake of example, let's say we're going to design a Neato-style (Fellowes) tray-card for the CD tray of a jewel box. The Neato template shows two tray-cards per sheet. Once your design is complete, you can elect to duplicate it in the second field or leave the remaining tray-card blank, depending upon how you prefer to print the finished result (see below).

Step 7: Manually duplicate the *outer* outline. Using the cybertool that lets you draw straight lines on your document, trace the four *outer* outlines—those which define the rectangular shape—of each tray-card template you've filled in. If the application software won't let you position your lines precisely *atop* the template guides, then create parallel lines *outside* but as *close* to them as possible. *Don't trace the inner lines, however.* Those are disposable aids that define subdivisions of the *visible* tray-card field, and should not appear on the finished document. And they'll disappear once you perform—

Step 8: Delete the pre-existing template outlines. Following click-and-delete protocols, locate and remove the factory-provided guidelines. *Now* there should be nothing left but your design and your duplicate *outer* lines. (If you've left the second tray-card blank, it should now be *entirely* invisible, and its half of the full-page view *entirely* empty.)

Step 9: Print copies as needed. If you've filled in both tray-cards, a single pass through the printer is, of course, all you need per sheet. If you've filled in only one template, rotate your printed pages 180 degrees, so that the bottom edges lead, and feed them through your printer a second time. Each printed sheet should now contain two perfectly positioned tray-cards.

Interlude before we continue: Except for tracing the outlines of the tray-card rectangle, you have so far done nothing "extra." I say this to emphasize what I meant by *"slightly* industrious." Now we proceed to the few chores that actually *do* require minor physical exertion and added steps in the normal tray-card-making chain.

Step 10: Create the final product with your paper trimmer. Using the outlines that you created, slice your inserts out of your printouts. Don't cut right *on* the outlines, or the inserts will be too big and you'll have to trim them again. Cut *inside* the outline, about an eighth of an inch. An average paper trimmer will let you cut through about five sheets simultaneously.

Step 11: Insert the insert. The only disadvantage your homemade tray-card has over one from a factory-made sheet is the lack of articulated "fold" lines, for the two thin title strips that will be displayed through the opposite narrow spines of the jewel case. But these are easily created. Hold any strip-edge of your insert flush with any spine-edge of the tray. Then, using a pointy but not-too-sharp tool that you can handle easily— say, the tip of an *empty* mechanical pencil (you don't want to puncture the paper)—and being careful to keep the insert steady and smooth against the plastic surface of the spine as you push down, "draw" an invisible line that tucks the insert securely into the right angle between the tray-spine and the tray backplate. Then do the same for the opposite side of the insert. After minimal practice, this takes barely more time than it would to fold along a manufactured crease. The end result is identical and looks every bit as professional.

Now let's review the math.

The average supply of pre-made inserts from the store will run you about thirty dollars. Prorated per sheet, you're spending something like fifty cents per insert.

On the other hand, once you change the rules in your favor: classy-looking cream-colored paper, which makes lovely inserts, goes for about five dollars a ream. A ream is five hundred sheets. Each sheet can yield two tray cards. Add the one-time expense of the paper trimmer, and that's forty dollars for one thousand inserts. Five dollars for every one thousand thereafter.

"Beating the system" is putting it mildly. . . .

Postscript

Two more quick notes on saving money:

1. You will need a CD labeling tool. The CD Stomper is probably the most popular, though Memorex and various other companies make them too. They're all pretty much the same, despite cosmetic differences. I won't describe the mechanism here, but it's a simple, spring-loaded device that lets you perfectly center the labels on your disks. All brands are typically overpriced, at roughly twenty to thirty dollars per unit, but it's worth the expense not to have to apply stickum with unaided hand-eye coordination. And as with the paper trimmer, you only have to buy the labeler once.

2. CD jewel boxes and cassette cases are also more cheaply bought in bulk. For my most recent demo, I created a two-sided tray-card layout that required completely clear jewel cases, which are not always readily available. Again 'Net trolling revealed a place where I could buy one hundred clear cases for about thirty dollars, plus shipping. The vendor is Sleeve City, 6610 Summer Ave Suite 101, Bartlett TN 38134, phone: (901) 380-4168, (M–F, 10:00 a.m.–6:00 p.m., CST), fax: (901) 380-4179 (24/7), website: www.sleevetown.com.

Happy and handsome demos to you all. . . .

SECTION FIVE: **RANDOM THOUGHTS, CODA, and APPENDICES**

AFTERWORD: RANDOM THOUGHTS

A FEW THINGS COME TO MIND THAT DIDN'T QUITE FIT IN ANY previous chapter, but seem worth mentioning . . .

HOMEWORK

There's a limit to what you can get in a book, no matter how thorough, or a classroom, no matter how brilliant the teacher/moderator; even seeing all the great musicals and memorizing their scores is not enough.

You have to sit down with those musicals yourself. Alone. Zen mode. The libretto in your lap, the CD or DVD in the tray, the mini-system remote within reach (because you'll want to pause, stop, repeat) and the answering machine screening unimportant calls. It's as much A Responsibility of the Job as facing the blank pad or filling the onscreen word-processor document.

All that you've read in these pages about the basic principles, about the importance of constantly deconstructing the musicals you see and know and learn . . . this is where it comes most crucially into play.

If you don't want to learn the literature . . . if indeed you don't *hunger* to learn it and claim doing so as one of life's primary joys . . . you shouldn't be writing musicals. It's like trying to be a surgeon without mastering *Gray's Anatomy,* or trying to be an aerospace engineer without studying math.

A number of seasons ago, Broadway (briefly) saw a show called *The Capeman.* The concept and the score were by no less a light than Paul Simon. And Simon was quite vocal and public about his unfamiliarity with musicals. And very specific in sending the message that he was gonna do something new, that he was gonna reinvent the wheel his way, that he was gonna break with tired tradition and show us all.

Needless to say, the show was a spectacular failure, and more than a little absurd even on its own terms.

Conversely, there's Trey Parker, co-creator (with Matt Stone) of the irreverent animated series *South Park*. He was likewise a first-time writer who, in association with Mark Shaiman, wrote a brilliant song-score for the motion picture *South Park: Bigger, Longer & Uncut,* which devastatingly parodied musical theatre conventions while also *sustaining itself* on its own terms. Its ever escalating irreverence made it ground-breaking and unique, but its success (and your giddy willingness to forgive its occasional craft-naïveté) lay in its total embrace of, affection for, *and intimate knowledge of* the canon.

Be smart about the homework. Do it as if your life depends on it.

Because as it happens . . .

LOCATION, LOCATION, LOCATION

Musical theatre develops primarily in New York City, by which I mean central Manhattan. At least in the United States. Even with those productions that appear for the first time regionally—if they feature the participation of even mildly experienced authorship, and/or any realistic prospect for coming "into town," the chances are the project and its team were somehow *assembled* in New York, and "went out" to try and work on the show removed from the mainstream gossip mill, with an eventual New York opening always in mind.

It may be possible to carve out some kind of career as a musical theatre dramatist outside of New York. (God knows, there are actors, directors, choreographers, playwrights, and other theatre artists who find themselves happy and productive and at times even overjoyed to be making their livings doing what they love, without the city's pressure and competitiveness.) But not if you ever intend to transcend "specialty" theatre or "novelty" shows. And not if you intend to work with and learn from the best of the musical theatre talent pool—*on a consistent, career-building basis.* Other towns and cities don't offer equivalent training, equivalent watering holes, equivalent opportunities . . . and, perhaps most important, don't really hold you to the equivalent high standard across the board.

This doesn't, ironically, mean that your most lucrative or fulfilling musicals will always *play* in New York City. Many successful tours have never come in. (On the high end: the Yeston-Kopit *Phantom* decided not to compete with the Lloyd Webber *Phantom* on Broadway, stuck to the regionals, made millions of dollars and as many devoted fans. On the workaday end: the Spencer-Barron TYA *Phantom* for Theatreworks/USA only pauses briefly in NYC during its cross-country tour of schools and family theatre venues, its fortunes and happy audiences more modest in number but nonetheless consistent and solid.) NYC, though, is where the alchemy usually happens to plant the creative seeds. Even those that flower elsewhere.

Despite the boom in electronic communications and media availability, NYC remains the center of the musical theatre universe, and it benefits composers, lyricists, and librettists to live there. Or in boroughs and environs close enough to get there easily. If they can.

Just as it's hard to write for the movies and television without moving to Hollywood, it's almost a contradiction in terms to pursue a musical dramatist's life without Manhattan as your principal environment and resource.

Weigh the evidence and decide where your life is happiest, and what you can accomplish from wherever that may be. But know that history tells you where the action is. And judge accordingly.

JUDGMENTS I

Ed Kleban once told a story about having presented a song at the BMI Workshop. When the class responded, he dutifully took his notes, and in his mind, silently dismissed the comment that came from "the class idiot." Walking down the street the next day, considering what he'd heard, he suddenly realized, "The idiot was right." It had taken him twenty-four hours to hear something vital. "You never know where the answer may come from," Ed said, "you have to be open to anyone. And when you have a show in previews, twenty-four hours is too long."

JUDGMENTS II

Criticism of work in progress from musical theatre people—even the most sensitive, informed, and insightful experts—tends to come at you fast, unsentimentally, candidly, and compactly. True enough, there are times when it also comes rudely, snobbishly, competitively, idiosyncratically—at moments even from A-list players, when they appear on panels—but *most* of the time, it's simply business as usual, with the assumption that everyone involved cares about the craft too much to mince words. The ultimate compliment, in a way, is faith in your desire to *get on with it.* Remember, as Kleban implied, if you're in previews and something doesn't work, you have to *fix* it, you have to fix it *fast,* as fast as you can *think,* constructively and without panic, and ain't no one gives a hoot in hell about your feelings. Theatre conditions its practitioners to lock, load, and fire.

And if you intend to write for the musical theatre, you have to learn to take it. Part of the trick is to be able to separate the suggestions thrown at you from the factors that *motivated* the suggestions, the diagnosis from the prescription. There may be times when the advice is 180 degrees wrong, but identifying the offensive problem will generally reveal the *right* strategy.

This is not to say that even ideally articulated criticism can't be unsettling, frustrating . . . even hurtful. We're all only human and there are a range of responses . . . but if you can hear what's being said to you, in spite of that, there is often, indeed usually, much to learn.

At times, such criticism can even be exhilarating. Sondheim, of course, is famous for being able to zero in with laser-sharp accuracy; when Maury Yeston, at the BMI Workshop, breaks a new song into its component parts and reassembles it to make it three times more effective, it's a display of dazzling problem-solving dexterity.

And right or wrong, as long as it's usefully provocative, as long as it helps you effectively change, refine or stand by your choices, it's an invigorating gift.

Learn to hear it.

Learn not to be intimidated by it.

Learn not to be (too terribly) defensive about it.

Learn how to ponder it.

Learn to give it constructively yourself.

And learn to love it.

CODA

Write well.
Respect the craft.
Create boldly.
See everything.
Remain open—but trust your gut.
Always care.
Stay passionate.
And survive.
If you're good—if you *make* yourself good—you can do it.
All of it.
Believe that.

Button.
Applaud here.

APPENDIX I
The Rave and the Mix
or:
Deconstruction in Action

I BECAME A DRAMA CRITIC AT THE AGE OF EIGHTEEN, WHEN I created a theatre column for my college paper. I don't recall how urgently I felt the need to be a critic per se, but I knew I wanted to make my living in the theatre *somehow,* and at least at the time, college papers qualified for press comps. But an unexpected thing happened: I grew addicted to the discipline of writing about what I saw—I realized that reviewing was giving me an education no class, comprehensive reading list, or research-driven independent study could begin to provide. I could literally feel my perception sharpening steadily, faster, as I understood more and more why things worked, why they didn't, and how all this understanding would affect my own work. When at last I *was* working professionally as a musical dramatist, the experience of walking "both sides of the street" was often epiphanal.

These revelations only became stronger and sharper over the years, through various subsequent critic gigs that continued pretty much nonstop, and culminated in 1996 when I uploaded the first edition of my theatre review website *Aisle Say.* Which at last allows me the freedom to consistently write drama criticism openly from the perspective of an insider—and the breathing room to occasionally compose leisurely, ruminative think-pieces, which not only explore the guts of a play, how it's built, but, when relevant, even its ramifications on theatre and craft in general. Musicals, of course, receive a lion's share of this kind of treatment.

Had I not written all those years of reviews, done all those thousands of deadlined analyses, I could not have written this book. Deconstructing a play is not fundamentally all that different from deconstructing a professional circumstance, once you have some experience at both. The same observational muscles are at work. It's all about reading the signs, and appraising what's been put before you.

That's why I wish there were room in the industry, plus time and circumstance, for *all* serious composers, lyricists, librettists to be drama critics *somewhere,* because the exercise of formal analysis and codification of your thoughts would prove as invaluable to you as it has to me. It is my hope that as you read what follows, you'll see why . . . and perhaps be inspired to keep a journal, or at least a book of notes, in which you can make your own observations, deconstructive analyses, appraisals. You'll find that the discipline of keeping the mental wheel well oiled, and the observational muscles in fighting trim equal to that of your writing muscles, pays off with powerful dividends.

And that brings us to the reviews that follow.

They're among the aforementioned think-pieces-*cum*-reviews from *Aisle Say,* as an example of that kind of study in action. One review is a rave, one is a mix—and *both* were singled out for admiration by members of the creative teams *and* their producers.

Their inclusion here—as with my reviews anywhere—is not to promulgate my often highly personal, idiosyncratic, *and even fallible* views, nor to incur your agreement, nor to put myself forth as some ultimate judge. None of which I'd even desire if I could achieve it. Well, not all the time, anyway.

The purpose is this, and *only* this: to start you thinking along similar analytical lines of your own.

Some musicals just seem to work every time. They bear examination, because the cause of their longevity provides many of the universal keys to the kingdom. When this review was uploaded, I shortly thereafter received an email whose author said it was "the best, most intelligent review of the show I've seen and I do not expect to read another that would change my mind. You hit so many nails on the head, I could barely get through it for the sound of all that hammering." And if that line sounds like vintage Larry Gelbart, it was indeed he who took the trouble to write so nicely.

Needless to say, I was pretty proud of that.

A FUNNY THING HAPPENED ON THE WAY
TO THE FORUM

Book by Larry Gelbart and Burt Shevelove
Music and Lyrics by Stephen Sondheim
Directed by Jerry Zaks
St. James Theatre

Not much in musical theatre is totally foolproof, even the stuff you *remember* as foolproof. I recall, as a young songwriter having just written a genuine showstopper of a number that was soon to be performed, popping off to one of my mentors that people would "have to try very hard to screw it up." His response was to caution me against such *hubris.* "I have," he said, "seen everything from 'Summertime' to the *Carousel* 'Soliloquy' come to naught . . . " And in the ensuing years since that sobering warning, so have I. The flawed concept of a director, an inappropriately cast performer, an inept choreographer, bad lighting . . . any *number* of things can mitigate against a moment working, let alone a show. That's only one of the reasons why the business of making musicals is so hard.

Yet there are two shows that seem to persist in being impervious to damage. The first, and most indestructible, is *Guys and Dolls,* revived on Broadway in 1992. Coming up a close second is *A Funny Thing Happened on the Way to the Forum,* currently in revival at the St. James Theatre. Interestingly, both revivals were directed by Jerry Zaks—and as if to illustrate the point, his *Guys and Dolls* was *wildly* misconceived, while his *Forum* is, for the most part right on target. And both revivals are/were stunning successes.

Probably the reason Zaks' *Forum* works so well is precisely the reason his *Guys and Dolls* was so infuriating. The latter is a warm show, and Zaks had leached the heart out of it, rendering it cold and comic book-y. Meanwhile, *Forum* is a piece for vaudevillians, based on the plays of Plautus. It isn't about heart, it's about belly-laughs. It's just fine on its own, and yet it welcomes almost anything you can do to embellish it. Subsequently, Zaks can throw the kitchen sink at it—which occasionally he does—and it cheerily cooperates with the excess.

Another reason *Forum* is so notable is the fact that it is the only musical farce ever produced that genuinely works. Indeed, librettists Burt Shevelove and Larry Gelbart, and then-young composer-lyricist Stephen Sondheim (for whom *Forum* was his first produced outing as composer/

lyricist and not just lyricist) spent eight years getting it right prior to its 1962 Broadway premiere. Why should musical farce be so difficult, and why should *Forum* be singular?

For one thing, farce is plot driven, musicals are character driven. Plot depends upon the machinations of events, dry information that is rarely (in and of itself) the stuff of songs. Characters, though, sing about feelings, ambitions, needs. Furthermore, even if you stop a farce plot to let the characters sing about themselves (as *Forum* does), you have to do it in such a way that you don't incur audience impatience when you bring the show to a halt. More still . . . the stakes have to be high enough to care about and be *worthy* of song. Your average Feydeau door-slammer is too light a confection to bear the weight of musicalization.

But *Forum*, despite its surface silliness, manages to be *about* something too. Taking place 200 years before the Christian era, on a street in ancient Rome, its hero is a slave, Pseudolous (Nathan Lane), desperate to buy his freedom (and the desire to be free is of course primal and *singable*). His master, young Hero (Jim Stanek) will *give* Pseudolous his freedom, if the slave can get him the one special girl he is in love with (you can sing about love too). Alas, this girl, a virgin named Philia (Jessica Boevers), resides within the house of Marcus Lycus (Ernie Sabella), a buyer and seller of courtesans. (Can Lycus sing about the virtues of his merchandise? But of course: and they can dance illustratively. Again, don't forget, this is not just a song about the pleasures of the flesh. This is a song about the pleasures of the flesh sung to a slave who can only purchase one girl for a boy who is in love so that the boy will give the slave his freedom. The brilliance of the show's structure is that it's all cumulative. But wait: it gets better.)

Philia is not for sale, though, having been promised to another buyer. Which means Pseudolous must trick Lycus into releasing Philia, must blackmail his fellow slave, the groveling Hysterium (Mark Linn-Baker) into using Hero's home to house the virgin while his parents—henpecked, lecherous Senex (Lewis J. Stadlen) and domineering Domina (Mary Testa)—are away. And which means Pseudolous must eventually outwit the aforementioned buyer, the notoriously hotheaded warrior, Miles Gloriosus (Cris Groenendaal). Because if he fails, Miles Gloriosus will kill him.

That's the secret. Right there. Aside from wit, taste and artistry, that arc illustrates the *structural* reason why *Forum* manages the hat trick no one else has ever pulled off. Because Pseudolous has a noble *character driven* objective—and because events get so tangled that the only alternative to getting what he wants . . . is death. Not only are the stakes high enough for the audience to care about . . . but the nobility of the hero keeps the farce from ever being mean-spirited.

An additional hallmark of this *particular* production is the mileage Zaks and company get out of knowing how familiar many of us are with the show; so there is some brilliant *schtick* right at the top, in the opening number "Comedy Tonight" which takes us totally by surprise, and throws off our expectations just enough to let us know that while we may be going to the same place we went last time, the ride itself will indeed, as the lyric says, be "something familiar, something peculiar."

Another interesting aspect of this production is how—by accident or design—the casting and playing styles acknowledge the passage of time.

Originally, as I say, *Forum* was a piece for vaudevillians, schtickmeisters from the Borscht Belt and comedy clubs, and extreme character types. Its original players included Mostel, Gilford, John Carradine, David Burns; an early 70s revival included Phil Silvers (the authors' original choice for the role), Nancy Walker, Mort Marshall and Carl Ballantine.

The above is an interesting list of players to contemplate for the following reason: They're all dead. That particular generation of comedy is almost entirely gone from the face of the earth, along with their particular sensibility and personality, preserved now only on record, on film . . . and in memory.[1]

So Zaks (and, I assume, Sondheim and Gelbart had a hand too) has cast a mostly younger group—younger in spirit anyway. They don't reflect the music hall and Burlesque sensibility because that isn't their heritage . . . so they bring a more contemporary energy to it. The energy of the well-made, low-comedy sitcom. The performances are streamlined and sleeker, the touch a bit lighter and a tad more cerebral. (As Hysterium—compare the image of craggy, smoky voiced old timer Jack Gilford with that of the current Hysterium: round-cheeked, baby-faced Mark-Linn Baker, aka "cousin" Larry Appleton on TV's "Perfect Strangers." The 1962 performance was one of ineradicable persona; the current one a brilliant character actor's turn—and one of the best things in the show.)

This is especially true of Nathan Lane's Pseudolous. Though he does bridge the generation gap with the most sublime mugging, pratfalls and double-whammy takes, he's also a naughtier, more contem-

---

1. I received another email about this piece too, from animation writer-director Mark Evanier (perhaps best known for his work on *Garfield*), who humorously informed me that Mr. Ballantine, who was one of his actively stalwart voiceover artists, would be very amused to learn of his passing. As of this April, 2005, interjection, Mr. Ballantine persists in being alive.

porary Pseudolous than Mostel or Silvers, reflecting his era in nuance. (E.g. in the opening number, he throws a doll, representing a baby, into the wings. At the performance I saw, he miscalculated: the doll bounced off the proscenium arch and back onto the stage. The audience reacted both to the symbolism—a doll-child hitting a wall still makes you think of a real child hitting a wall—and to the gaffe. What would Lane do? He picked up the doll, looked out into the house and said, "No babies were harmed in tonight's performance." Huge applause, he flung the doll offstage and continued. What's notable here is that the ad lib—a recognizable variation of "No animals were harmed in the filming of tonight's episode"—is a *TV* ad lib, reflecting our culture and the way we live now.)

The casting falls a bit short at times. Mary Testa doesn't have a handle on Domina, so she works it too hard and the laboring makes the role less funny. Also, Cris Groenendaal, though physically right for the warrior Miles, is miscast. The role seems to want a true baritone, while Mr. Groenendaal is more of a tenor, and thus his songs, such as "Bring Me My Bride" sound too light of timbre to be fully effective. But the real reason he's miscast is that he's not particularly funny. He has a sweetness and a sense of humor that have served him in other roles—but a flair for comedy, for timing, for making a joke land: that, alas, no.

All the others, though, even the ingenues, have a no-nonsense sense of nonsense. Set and costume designer Tony Walton has contributed numerous delightful sight gags, Rob Marshall silly—and for the courtesans sexy—choreography; and there are new orchestrations by Jonathan Tunick. Often, Mr. Tunick takes his lead from the originals, by Sid Ramin and Irwin Kostal, which used no high strings, a subtle homage to the hard, low comedy of the evening. But Mr. Tunick occasionally departs from their template, doing something more elegant, and indeed bringing violins into the mix. The sound is not a radical departure—he hasn't rearranged Mr. Sondheim's music, merely re-orchestrated—and might not be right for every production; but it fits the sensibility of *this* production quite nicely.

The Sondheim score is as indestructible as the show itself; in its last Broadway revival, it picked up two songs ("Echo Song" and "Farewell") and dropped two ("Pretty Little Picture" and "That'll Show Him"). This version goes back to the original 1962 song roster, though "Pretty Little Picture" is eliminated. (It's my favorite song in the score, but I must admit that somehow, in the Zaks staging, it would seem superfluous and slow down the antics.)

The Gelbart-Shevelove libretto is also mind-bogglingly fresh. I thought I heard interpolated lines in this revival, went back to the original script and . . . lo and behold, there they were, so vital as to seem anachronistic thirty-five years later.

All of us who write musicals want to write a hit. . . . Imagine, though, what it must be like to write a warhorse.

In any event, get yourself down to the St. James Theatre. Where for two and a half hours you can at least *ride* one. A foolproof one. With the fools to prove it. . . .

There are musicals that some people love and some people hate. But there are often compelling reasons for the polarization, and they tend to be rooted in the approach the creative team take to their storytelling.

Though Titanic *proved to have a very decent Broadway run (804 performances, nearly a full two years), and went on to win four Tony awards (musical, score, book, and orchestrations), it was kept, yes, afloat by word of mouth and the novelty of its own subject matter. For most of the major reviews had been dismissive, some even using the theme of a sunken ship to be glib, in an obvious and destructive manner.*

Thus I learned, in several surprising in-person encounters, that this review, though mixed, was greatly appreciated by the authors and the producers— taken by them as something of a huge relief from the onslaught—because it took the show seriously and examined it in rigorous depth.

I was proud of that too, of course, but also a little sad. As a critic, taking a sincere effort seriously is part of my job. And no less than the show deserved—from anyone. Bear that in mind as you view and deconstruct shows in turn . . .

TITANIC

Story and Book by Peter Stone
Music and Lyrics by Maury Yeston
Directed by Richard Jones
Lunt-Fontanne Theatre

One of the most frequent gripes I hear (and to be honest, have) about theatre reviews is how a critic will sometimes mislead you with a lot of verbiage at the top and not tell you what s/he *really* thinks until two-thirds of the way through the notice.

This is one of those reviews.

Bear with me. I have to do it this way, because my response to *Titanic* is not simple or straightforward. And I rather suspect yours won't be either . . .

* * * * * * * * *

When Peter Stone wrote the book for *1776* he had to contend with many of the same structural challenges that come built into his latest, *Titanic*—in collaboration with composer-lyricist Maury Yeston and director Richard Jones.

Both are, of course, based on historical incidents: *1776* about the creation and signing of the Declaration of Independence, the latter about the tragic sinking of the famous ship. So we know, as we take our seats, how each'll turn out.

1776 begins with the burning passion of its angry hero, John Adams, to see America free of British tyranny. But so contrary is his nature to his goal that his colleagues in Congress—even those sympathetic to the cause—won't even *debate* American independence because his bullish tenacity so pisses them off. That's where the drama begins. There are many characters in *1776*, most of them congressmen, most of them important in one way or another, more than usual to keep track of even in a big musical—and yet you do . . . because Adams is the hub. They are satellites who relate to *him,* rather than to the abstraction of "independence"—more specifically, he *personifies* the abstraction. And that relationship, complete with worthy and intelligent opposition (led by conservative John Dickinson) is so contentious as to demystify the historical aura of "great men." We become so caught up in the idiosyncrasies of these characters, the intricacy of the battle, and the roiling, deeply human interplay between the factions, that as the odds against Adams mount—

—we forget that we know the outcome. And we actually begin to doubt.

Titanic has no main character as such. Our first image is a show curtain that features a blueprint rendering of the ship as viewed from stem to stern. The curtain rises, and alone onstage is Thomas Andrews (Michael Ceveris), the man who designed the ship, standing on the dock, near the WHITE STAR LINE gangplank, holding—we assume—the same blueprint . . . comparing his handiwork to the great *thing* he gapes at, which seems to be located just offstage. This gives his character the potential to be in the Adams "slot," if you stretch a point . . . but unlike Adams, who has to change the world, Andrews' work is done when we meet him. The ship *has* been built, it *is* going to launch, and the only path he can travel is one that goes from elation . . . to worry . . . to regret. His submissive, milquetoast nature gives little hope of anything else. So we realize that he will not carry us through the evening.

As other characters gather for the opening scene, passengers and crew, they too react to the unseen ship—her majestic size and scope, the thrill of boarding her . . . but as the ship is merely a symbolic reflection of their individual hopes and dreams about what will or may await them upon journey's end, it is defined as an abstraction—and we start to understand, despite the impressive and intricate choral singing of the huge opening number, that interpersonal relationships are not the order of the day. Within minutes, we realize that *Titanic* intends to feature a collage of lives, a series of recurring, and slowly developing, dramatic snapshots. We'll get to know some of the characters better than others, of course—among about two dozen, the Captain (John Cunningham), a venal White Star executive (David Garrison), the elderly Strauses of first class (Larry Keith and Alma Cuervo), an unmarried pregnant girl from Ireland (Jennifer Piech), a coal stoker (Brian d'Arcy James), a radioman (Martin Moran), a celebrity-struck 2nd classer (Victoria Clark) and her suffering but tolerant husband (Bill Buell)—but because they are not larger-than-life characters (à la *1776*), and because that knowledge comes in small, cumulative doses, rather than in broad brushstrokes . . . we don't bond with them. Like them, yes, most. But become invested—? Only mildly, and only midway through the second act, which is when some are finally rounded out enough to seem more than essences and archetypes. The fact that the stories never cross-pollinate keeps the dramatic issues from becoming terribly "hot" . . . and renders even the issue of life and death to be one of academic rather than visceral interest. We are curious to know who will survive—but one answer would do as well as another. And the outcome is never in doubt. Nor do we find ourselves saddened by, or wishing against, that inevitability.

Final *1776* comparison. What further roots your familiarity with the many characters and issues at stake *there* is the dramatic centralization. About 85% of the play takes place in the Continental Congress. Where the various representative have nesting places. Lewis Morris of New York occupies that chair *there*, Samuel Chase of Maryland is *here*. Furthermore, Peter Stone devised a brilliant addition to the set (brilliantly

realized in Jo Mielziner's original design), which was the one accoutre-
ment that wasn't a historical reality. But it is the heart and soul of the
show's clarity.

The scoreboard.

It hung on the back wall, a bit right of center. Three columns, each with
thirteen rows. First column labeled YEA. Second column a row of
bleached wood tiles, each sporting the name of a different colony. Third
column labeled NAY. Whenever a vote was taken, Congressional Secre-
tary Charles Thompson reached up with a hooked pole, fit it into a hole
in the appropriate tile and—*whap*—slid it into the appropriate column. If
ever you forgot where things stood, you merely shifted your eyes for an
instant refresher. This, among other things, made the *setting* as much a
character as any of the people onstage.

Even though most of *Titanic*'s action takes place on the ship, it takes
place *all over* the ship, and designer Stewart Laing keeps the stew varied,
even cleverly altering recurring settings in the second act as the ship begins to tilt. Nonetheless, this means that the set, like the show's
construction, functions in a leitmotivic way. It doesn't—no pun intended—anchor you. The multiple storylines don't become confusing,
precisely, but you have to be especially alert to keep track of all the players, until they become familiar. Also, unlike the *1776* set, *Titanic*'s more
often than not lacks physical depth. The concept behind it seems to be
one of letting audience imagination fill out grand details by presenting
variations of blueprint mapping—as foreshadowed by the show curtain.
Subsequently, almost every exterior scene is set against a symbolic flat;
and almost every interior scene is a mere slice of the stage, viewed
through a panel cut into a black flat on any one of three levels, as if it were
a cross-section. The consequential straight-line/cramped-space staging,
bereft of geometric variation, tends to restrict the mind's eye from filling
in detail, just as it often restricts movement. Which means, of course, that
the Titanic *never* feels like a character. It is unquestionably a big implacable *thing*—but it has no personality of its own.

Okay. That's the misleading verbiage. Now here's what I really think.

Having said all that, how well does *Titanic* work?

Better than it has any right to. And here's why: none of it appears acci-
dental. Whatever the actual gestation process may have entailed (and for
all the people I know who are involved, I have surprisingly little knowledge of any of it), the net result of the frozen show is one of a high-octane

creative team acting in concert. I doubt very much, for example, that Mr. Stone didn't think about *1776* himself and make these same comparisons as he was outlining the structure. And I'm certain that if these arguments were presented to him, he would say, "Yes, you're right about some things, but *Titanic* had to be done in *this* fashion because—." And then he'd tell you why those very conscious choices were made, as opposed to others. And he might even be right.

The innate pretension of the show—I don't mean that as a pejorative—and its ambition add to the sturdiness of the vessel (and that pun *is* intended). *How are they going to solve* this? you wonder, *how will they deal with* that? (You tend to *think* about those solutions as they're presented, which is unfortunate, but that makes them no less fascinating.)

The cast is swell, the direction is clean, the hydraulics work well, sometimes even impressively—

—and most importantly, Maury Yeston's score gives the piece a palpable soul. Even in its more lighthearted moments, Yeston's music never loses the æsthetic of epic consequence. It paints its varied dramatic moods with uncanny accuracy and it is almost always ravishingly lovely (and orchestrator Jonathan Tunick knows just how to put it in its best light). The astonishing choral writing alone is, as they say, worth the price. As for Yeston's lyrics—

—per usual, they are technically more often only sufficient unto the task than they are inspired . . . but in terms of character psychology, setting the right tone, adding some flesh to the cameo bones . . . it is some of his best and smartest work.

Given the way the structure of the show keeps you at a distance, the score isn't set up to be as moving as it wants to be . . . perhaps isn't allowed to be as moving as it *is* . . . I'm not sure about that. I *am* certain that we'll all appreciate the emotional nuances more when its forthcoming album puts it into high relief, away from the trappings of the physical production that surrounds it so coolly—and that the album will wear well upon repeated listenings.

In the end, *Titanic* is, like its namesake, a grand idea with many built-in flaws. The difference is, unlike its namesake, it stays afloat.

It's never dull.

It goes by at a clip.

And whatever else may be true, it's like an iceberg coming hard at you off the port bow, and you cannot take your eyes—or ears—off it . . .

APPENDIX II
Grants and Development Programs

GRANTS

There aren't many grants for musical theatre writers, but there are a handful of prestigious awards to go after. Those listed in this section are not the only ones, but they are the major annuals that cause the most flurry and feverish preparation among the community of aspiring and emerging musical dramatists as deadlines draw nigh. (Contact information is on page 192.)

The **Richard Rodgers Foundation** gives three awards: *Development Awards*, which fund staged readings of a new musical; *Workshop Awards*, which fund workshop productions; and *Production Awards*, which supplement full productions. Each successive award is worth more money toward staging the musical—money that goes to a New York City–based not-for-profit theatre willing to dedicate its resources—and to the musical's author(s).

The drawback is that the production monies must be used within a year from the time they're allotted or they'll be withdrawn, and it's up to you to find the NFP theatre. (Once you find the theatre, if there are scheduling problems, an extension can often be worked out.) Since the award contract clearly stipulates that the NFP venue can get no continuing interest in the winning piece as a result of any Rodgers-funded event (as opposed to any further, independent development they may nurture, which is another matter), this is not always easy, and certain managing directors have accordingly (sometimes not even very covertly) juggled their books to siphon off some of the production money for their theatre's general use. This aspect of the award, winners agree, has been overdue for renovation for quite some time.

That said, Rodgers-awarded musicals get a certain amount of attention because of the automatic pedigree conferred by a blue-ribbon jury that is headed by Stephen Sondheim and has included Richard Maltby, Jr., Lynn Ahrens, Sheldon Harnick, and others of similarly high stature.

The Rodgers Award is also probably the most fairly judged and least susceptible to political bias of any—not because the others are less honorable, but because the Rodgers process provides unique checks and balances. In most other competitions, submissions are *divided* among individual screeners, who determine which applicants move up to the next level of judgment—but in the Rodgers process each of four screeners reviews *all* submissions, and the submissions are "blind" (no bylines). The screeners write brief reports and can give four possible grades: *yes, maybe yes, maybe no,* and *no.* All it takes is *one yes* vote for a piece to get kicked upstairs for the star jury's consideration, on the premise that if only *one* person finds a submission intriguing enough to pass on, there may well be something unusually special about it.

Only full drafts of scripts are accepted. Synopses required. Demos not to exceed forty-five minutes (though no decent submission has ever been penalized for doing so within reason). Submit only when you're sure you're ready to, because the Rodgers will not consider the same project twice, even if heavily revised. (This does not apply to winning projects, which may submit for any higher awards that may be applicable.)

The Gilman and Gonzalez-Falla Theater Foundation is funded by this dear and incredibly generous philanthropic couple, Celso Gonzalez-Falla, a businessman, and his wife, Sondra Gilman, a renowned photographer and author, who care passionately about the musical theatre and the new writers trying to create it. Each year they—and their own blue-ribbon panel, which has included notables such as Jerry Herman—give one or two writers (and/or writing teams) a $25,000 grant to enhance career and living expenses; and a few more commendation grants ($1,000 each) to runners-up. Winners become, in a sense, members of Sondra and Celso's extended family, to whom they continue to lend support.

Though you formally win for your given year's submission, the award and continued support are often granted based upon cumulative merit, continuous work over a period of years. Sondra and Celso keep tabs on promising candidates.

To be eligible for the award, the artist must have had one musical produced in the United States in a commercial or professional non-profit theatre.

The Kleban Foundation Awards. Ed Kleban, lyricist of *A Chorus Line*, and posthumous composer-lyricist of *A Class Act* (the musical sorta kinda about his life), bequeathed $100,000 per year to go to a deserving lyricist, and another $100,000 to a deserving librettist. (He thought composers had enough awards available to them.) This award is for career enhancement and for living expenses, to be used as the winner sees fit. Occasionally winners have tied, and in those years, the pot is split.

This is among the most sought-after awards because it buys an aspiring writer a lot of freedom for a considerable period of time.

Lyricists submit five to eight lyrics with setups for context, plus matching demo recording. Librettists submit one complete two-act musical or two complete acts of two different musicals (enhanced, I would recommend, by synopses of the missing acts).

Qualifications:

1. A work by the applicant has previously been produced on a stage or in a workshop performance.
2. The applicant is or has been a member or an associate of a professional musical workshop or theatre group, i.e., ASCAP, BMI Theatre Workshop or the Dramatists Guild Musical Theater Development Program.

The Jonathan Larson Awards. The mandate of the *Larson Foundation*, created by his family in memory of the author of *Rent*, is "to provide encouragement and financial assistance to composers, lyricists and bookwriters as well as nonprofit producing companies with a commitment to supporting the work of new musical theatre projects and musical theatre artists." Its application process includes several sometimes complex steps and can include a request for your financial records, as need can also be a factor.

(For the record: I have screened for the Rodgers Awards and won a production award in 2002 for *The Fabulist*. I won a 2000 Kleban award for lyrics from *The Apprenticeship of Duddy Kravitz*, *The Fabulist*, and the Theatreworks/USA *Les Misérables*. I received two Gilman and Gonzalez-

Falla commendation grants: one in 1996 for my Theatreworks/USA *Phantom of the Opera*, one in 2002 for *The Fabulist*—as well as enhancements of $5,000 toward the making of the *Phantom* album and $10,000 toward the further development of *The Fabulist*. To paraphrase a famous Red Buttons routine: "Never got a Larson.")

The Richard Rodgers Awards
c/o The American Academy
of Arts and Letters
633 W 155th St.
New York, NY 10032-7599
(212) 368-5900

The Kleban Foundation Awards
The Kleban Foundation, Inc.
c/o New Dramatists
424 West 44th Street
New York, NY 10036
(212) 757-6960
newdramatists@newdramatists.org
www.newdramatists.org/
kleban_award.htm

The Gilman and Gonzalez-Falla Musical Theater Awards
c/o The Gilman and Gonzalez-
Falla Theater Foundation
109 East 64th Street
New York, NY 10021
Phone: (212) 734-8011
Fax: (212) 734-9606
www.ggftheater.org

The Jonathan Larson Awards
Jonathan Larson Performing Arts
Foundation
P.O. Box 672, Prince St. Station
New York, NY 10012
Phone: (212) 529-0814
Fax: (212) 253-7604
jlpaf@aol.com
www.jlpaf.org/index.html

DEVELOPMENT

There are also several opportunities for project development and show-casing of work in progress. Here are three of the most prominent ones to check out:

The National Alliance for Musical Theatre (NAMT)
520 Eighth Avenue, Suite 301, 3rd Floor
New York, NY 10018
Phone: (212) 714-6668
Fax: (212) 714-0469
info@namt.net
www.namt.net

O'Neill Music Theater Conference
305 Great Neck Road
Waterford, CT 06385
Phone: (860) 443-5378 extension 301
Fax (860) 443-9653
musictheater@theONEILL.org

NYC Musical Theatre Festival
1697 Broadway, Suite 902
New York, NY 10019
Phone: (212) 664-0979
Fax: (212) 664-0978
info@nymf.org
www.nymf.org

APPENDIX III
A Better-Than-Average Shelf Life
or:
The "Additional Reading" List

I HAVE A BIAS CONCERNING BOOKS ABOUT WRITING. WRITING musicals or anything else. I tend to think they're not worth a rodent's rump unless they're penned by people who actually *do* the kind of writing they're writing *about.*

For a living.

I suppose there are rare exceptions, and I won't tell you not to be open-minded; but if you hold to the "no civilians" philosophy, it sure steers you clear of myth, urban legend, academic posturing, and just plain quackery.

I've also found that a good book about the craft of storytelling—*any* kind of storytelling—is of value to writing musical theatre, because there always seem to be aspects of one craft that can be transmuted to aspects of another; things that one craft asks you to think about that can *solve problems* in another.

Following, then, is my suggested, short "additional reading" list. The range of the list is personal, eclectic, and hardly comprehensive. But these are the works that have meant the most to *me* over the years, providing hard knowledge, vigorous inspiration, and flat-out joy, for they're all great reads and worth revisiting every so often.

The TV Scriptwriter's Handbook, by Alfred Brenner (Writer's Digest Books, 1980)
Libretto writing bears a much closer resemblance to screenplay and teleplay writing than it does to straight play writing, because of its economy and relative brevity, and Mr. Brenner's handbook is a bible for matters of

construction. The author, an Emmy winner, penned scripts for 1960s–1970s shows like *Harry O, The Bold Ones,* and *Mannix*—but, speaking as a fellow who grew up on such shows, I swear to you those old-school guys could be *very* hip. And Brenner is among the hippest. Included in the book is a full teleplay he wrote for the medical drama *Ben Casey.*

How to Write Best Selling Fiction, by Dean Koontz (Writer's Digest Books, 1981)
Out of print, and used copies go for over $100. Worth every penny, if you can afford it, but if that's gulp-inducing, any good library system should eventually be able to locate a copy.

The popular master suspense novelist discusses the craft and the business of being a commercial novelist in entertaining, to-the-point chapters. The section on pages 201–205, about omniscient and modified omniscient viewpoints—especially the warning against internal point-of-view shifts within sections—is alone worth having, and can be used to pinpoint trouble spots in lyrics and song construction . . . especially story songs and long, complex songs that need to cover a lot of narrative ground from different perspectives.

The Complete Book of Scriptwriting, by J. Michael Straczynski (revised and expanded edition, Writer's Digest Books, 1996)
The redoubtable creator/auteur of the television series *Babylon 5* takes you through the protocols and principles of the craft and the biz. Believe *nothing* he tells you about playscript formatting—he's not a theatre man, he's a Hollywood man, and he passes off publishing layout as rehearsal script standard, which is hogwash. But when he talks about construction, character and how to work like a pro, he's at the top of his game.

(The original edition, copyrighted 1982, is not to be sneezed at if you come across it first; but the "revised and expanded" is nearly two hundred pages longer, and includes a full *Babylon 5* teleplay as one of its appendices.)

Making Musicals, by Tom Jones (Limelight Editions, 1998)
The lyricist-librettist of *The Fantasticks!, 110 in the Shade, I Do! I Do!, Philemon, Celebration,* and others presents a self-described "informal introduction to the world of musical theatre." The first half of the book is a history of the form, the second half a look at the craft. The beginning writer, especially one still learning the literature, is likely to find this

modest book fun and informative; the more advanced and show-literate the writer, however, the milder and less revelatory this book will seem.

But it's a volume worth knowing, because Tom Jones is one of the Great Survivors, and, to the best of my knowledge, he's the first of the genuine, modern book musical practitioners to commit his thoughts on the craft to a full book between covers.

The Season: A Candid Look at Broadway, by William Goldman, (Harcourt Brace, 1969, Bantam Books paperback, 1970, current edition reissued by Limelight Editions, 1984)
A legendary book that has been a pervasive educator, provocateur, and influence on several generations of theatre people, Goldman's sassy, colloquial survey of a single season on Broadway and what makes it tick (1967–68) has only recently started to show its age, now that the technological/communications boom has revolutionized the way theatre as a commodity is presented to the public. But Goldman's examination of the *creative* and *collaborative* processes and personnel, virtues and foibles, is as vital now as it was over three decades ago.

The success Goldman found as a novelist (*Boys & Girls Together, Soldier in the Rain, No Way to Treat a Lady,* others) and later as a screenwriter (*Butch Cassidy and the Sundance Kid, The Hot Rock, Harper, Misery, All the President's Men,* adaptations of his novels *The Princess Bride, Marathon Man, Magic* to name but a few) eluded him as a theatre dramatist (he cowrote the libretto to the musical *A Family Affair* [music by John Kander, direction taken over for New York by Hal Prince] and cowrote the military service comedy *Blood, Sweat and Stanley Poole,* both with his late brother James—the latter best remembered for *The Lion in Winter* and *Follies*) but still, he delivers *The Season* as an insider going for broke with understanding, empathy, righteous rage, joy, sorrow, and dynamic passion—and the result is a notoriously compulsive read.

(You might think about adding to the list Goldman's two famous books about screenwriting—*Adventures in the Screen Trade* and its sequel, *Which Lie Did I Tell?*—as well as his anthologies, published by Applause Books: *Four Screenplays* and *Five Screenplays,* which contain his most major works for the movies, plus essays on each. Published separately by Applause, but also introduced by vigorously informative essays, are Goldman's screenplays for *The Ghost and the Darkness* and *Absolute Power,* the latter of which provides an unforgettable deconstruction of the adaptation process that produced a script from David Baldacci's novel.)

Letters from an Actor, by William Redfield (1967, various editions)
Not really a book on writing per se, but a thoughtful book that can *inform* writing enormously.

In the early sixties, there was a rehearsal-dress production of *Hamlet* that played Broadway. A damn near all-star affair, and a bona-fide EVENT, it starred Richard Burton and was directed by John Gielgud. One of its co-stars was the late William Redfield, a ubiquitous and fine character actor of the period (who played Rosencrantz—even the cameo players were significant) and he chronicled the experience in a journal, which he wrote as if it were a series of letters to a friend.

The resultant book, aside from being an invaluable look into the mind of a working actor (these are the cats who put their ass on the line for you, it helps to know what makes 'em tick), is also brilliantly observed and written with often startling, perspective-altering insight.

It is worth noting too that the production was audio-recorded by Columbia records, and filmed as well—the latter now available on DVD. It's quite an experience to read Redfield's excellent book and then hear or watch the actual production, as a kind of "living" testament to his reports and impressions.

The Glass Teat (1970), *The Other Glass Teat* (1975), *Harlan Ellison's Watching (1989),* by Harlan Ellison
The angry, furiously funny bantam who in his youth was known as the *enfant terrible* of speculative fiction, and the winner of numerous awards for his teleplays and short stories, laces into television (the *Teat*s) and cinema (*Watching*), by way of examining American culture in general, in these reprints of devastating essays he wrote for the *Los Angeles Free Press* and others. He rants, raves, and ruminates about the business he knows from the inside, and what makes his books of media criticism valuable to a musical dramatist is that they represent some of the finest deconstructionist analyses ever to see print. And they are written with a muscular, infectious energy that will slam its way into your bloodstream like a mainline hit. The mere act of reading him makes you a better writer. As well as a smarter one. (His essays on other wide-ranging subjects can be found in *An Edge in My Voice, Sleepless Nights in the Procrustean Bed* and—one that I would not recommend as an introduction, because it's something of a dated indulgence for him—*The Harlan Ellison Hornbook.*)